First World War
and Army of Occupation
War Diary
France, Belgium and Germany

8 DIVISION
Divisional Troops
Divisional Trench Mortar Batteries
25 May 1916 - 31 October 1918

WO95/1696

The Naval & Military Press Ltd
www.nmarchive.com
Published in association with The National Archives

Published by

The Naval & Military Press Ltd

Unit 10 Ridgewood Industrial Park,

Uckfield, East Sussex,

TN22 5QE England

Tel: +44 (0) 1825 749494

www.naval-military-press.com

www.nmarchive.com

This diary has been reprinted in facsimile from the original. Any imperfections are inevitably reproduced and the quality may fall short of modern type and cartographic standards.

© **Crown Copyright**
Images reproduced by permission of The National Archives, London, England, 2015.

Contents

Document type	Place/Title	Date From	Date To
Heading	1696 Code Es 3 1.30 1 Hour 40 Min		
Heading	8th Division Trench Mortar Batteries May 1916-Oct 1918		
Heading	8th Div. I.Corps. War Diary M/s Trench Mortar Battery. 25th May 1916 To 8th August 1916.		
Miscellaneous	To Officer In Record A.G.'s Office Base.	30/10/1917	30/10/1917
Heading	War Diary From May 25th. 16. To Aug. 8th. 1916		
War Diary	Albert	25/05/1916	19/07/1916
War Diary	Bethune	22/07/1916	08/08/1916
War Diary	In The Field	08/08/1916	08/08/1916
Heading	8th,Division V.W.X.Y.Z. T. M. Battery. August, 1916.		
Heading	Confidential 8th Divisional Artillery. War Diary of V,W,X,Y,Z, T.M Batteries From 1-8-16 To 31-8-16. (Volume 1) With Appendices Nos. None		
War Diary	Sailly La Bourse	01/08/1916	31/08/1916
Heading	8th, Division. W/8, Heavy T. M. Battery. September, 1916.		
Heading	8th Divisional Artillery. War Diary of W/8 Heavy T.M. Battery From 1-9-16 To 90-9-16 (Volume 4) With Appendices Nos. One		
Heading	W/8 Heavy Trench Mortar Battery. September 1916.		
War Diary	Sailly La Bourse	01/09/1916	30/09/1916
War Diary		29/09/1916	29/09/1916
War Diary	8th, Division. W/8, Heavy T. M. Battery. October, 1916.		
Heading	Confidential War Diary W/8 Heavy Trench Mortar Battery. From. 01.10.16.-31.10.16. Vol II.		
War Diary	In The Field.	01/10/1916	31/10/1916
Heading	8th, Division. W/8 Heavy T. M. Battery. November, 1916.		
Heading	Confidential War Diary of W/8 Heavy Trench Mortar Battery From 24th 11/16----30/11/16 Volume III		
War Diary	In The Field	03/11/1916	29/11/1916
Heading	8th, Division. W/8, Heavy T. M. Battery. December, 1916.		
Heading	Confidential War Diary W/8 Heavy Trench Mortar Battery From 1st.12.16. To 31.12.16 Vol III		
War Diary	In The Field	01/12/1916	31/12/1916
Heading	8th, Division. X/8 Medium T. M. Battery. September, 1916.		
Heading	Confidential 8th Divisional Artillery. War Diary of X/8 Medium Trench Mortar Bty. From 1-9-16 To 30-09-16. (Volume 1) With Appendices Nos. None		
War Diary	Vermelles	01/09/1917	30/09/1917
Heading	8th Division. X/8, T. M. Battery. October, 1916.		
Heading	Confidential War Diary Of X/8 T.M.B. Volume (II) From Oct 1st 1916 To Oct 31st 1916.		
War Diary	Hohen Zollern Re Doubt And Right	01/10/1916	31/10/1916
Heading	8th, Division. X/8, T. M. Battery. November, 1916.		

Heading	Confidential. War Diary of X/8 T.M.B. 31st/10/16 To 1st/12/16 Vol. III		
War Diary	Mannsel Camp	01/11/1916	30/11/1916
Heading	8th, Division. X/B, T. M. Battery. December, 1916.		
Heading	Confidential War Diary of X/8 Trench. Mortar Battery From 1-12-16 To 31-12-16 Vol (3)		
War Diary	Line Of March	01/12/1916	02/12/1916
War Diary	Andain Ville	03/12/1916	09/12/1916
War Diary	Line Of March	10/12/1916	10/12/1916
War Diary	Liomer	11/12/1916	31/12/1916
Heading	8th, Division. 23rd, T. M. Battery. 17/8/16 to 31/8/16.		
Heading	23rd T. M. Battery. War Diary 17-8-16-31-8-16.		
War Diary	In The Field	17/08/1916	31/08/1916
Heading	8th, Division. 24th, T. M. Battery. August, 1916.		
War Diary	Fosse 9 Annequin	01/08/1916	05/08/1916
War Diary	Beuvry	06/08/1916	07/08/1916
War Diary	Hulluch Sector Trenches	08/08/1916	14/08/1916
War Diary	Novelles Billet Fouquereuil:	15/08/1916	22/08/1916
War Diary	Vermelles	23/08/1916	23/08/1916
War Diary	Honenzollen Trenches.	24/08/1916	31/08/1916
Heading	25th, T. M. Battery. August, 1916.		
Heading	War Diary of The 25 Light Trench Mortar Battery		
War Diary	Vermelles	01/08/1916	04/08/1916
War Diary	Honen-zollern Section	05/08/1916	06/08/1916
War Diary	Rouquer-veil	07/08/1916	16/08/1916
War Diary	Quarries Section	17/08/1916	31/08/1916
Heading	8th, Division. 8th, T. M. Battery. June, 1916.		
War Diary	Noote Boom Nr Berthen	01/06/1916	11/06/1916
War Diary	Reninghelst	11/06/1916	11/06/1916
War Diary	Trenches 9 To 28	12/06/1916	21/06/1916
War Diary	St Martuis au last	22/06/1916	30/06/1916
Heading	8th, Division. Y/8, Medium T. M. Battery. September, 1916.		
Heading	Confidential War Diary of Y/8 Medium Trench Mortar Battery From 1.9.16. To 30.9.16 Volume I		
War Diary	Hohenzollern Sector	01/09/1916	03/09/1916
War Diary	Gun G in Cromwell Rd		
War Diary	Gun F In Left Boyan		
War Diary	Huhenzollern Sector	04/09/1916	04/09/1916
War Diary	E Gun Off Burts Allay (in OB1).	04/09/1916	04/09/1916
War Diary	F Gun In Left Boyan Gun Of Auamy Alley		
War Diary	Huhenzollern Sector	05/09/1916	05/09/1916
War Diary	E Gun In OB 1	06/09/1916	06/09/1916
War Diary	E Gun In OB.		
War Diary	Huhenzollern Sector	07/09/1916	08/09/1916
War Diary	E in OB, Off Barts Alley	09/09/1916	09/09/1916
War Diary	F In Left Bayan	09/09/1916	09/09/1916
War Diary	G In Cromwell Rd of Quany Alley	09/09/1916	09/09/1916
War Diary	Hohenzollern Sector	10/09/1916	22/09/1916
War Diary	Hohenzollern Redoubt	24/09/1916	28/09/1916
War Diary	Hohenzollern Sector	29/10/1916	30/10/1916
Heading	8th, Division. Y/8, Medium T. M. Battery. October, 1916.		
Heading	Confidential War Diary. Of Y/8 Medium Trench Mortar Battery From 1.10.16 To 31.10.16 Volume I		
War Diary	Hohenzollern Sector	01/10/1916	03/10/1916

War Diary	Hohenzollern Redoubt.	04/10/1916	08/10/1916
War Diary	Hohenzollern Redoubt.	09/10/1916	31/10/1916
Heading	8th, Division. V/8, Heavy T. M. Battery. September, 1916.		
Heading	Confidential 8th Divisional Artillery. War Diary of V/8 Heavy Trench Mortar Battery From 1-9-16 To 30-9-16 (Volume 1)		
Miscellaneous			
War Diary	Sailly La Bourse	01/09/1916	30/09/1916
Heading	8th, Division. V/8, Heavy T. M. Battery. October. 1916.		
Heading	Confidential War Diary of V/8 Heavy Trench Mortar Battery. From 01/10/16 31/10/16 Volume II		
War Diary	In The Field	01/10/1916	31/10/1916
Heading	8th, Division. V/8, Heavy T. M. Battery. November, 1916.		
War Diary	Confidential War Diary of V/8 Heavs Trench Mortar Battery From 11/11/16 23/11/16 Volume III		
War Diary	In The Field	01/11/1916	23/11/1916
Heading	8th Div. I. Corps. War Diary W/8 Heavy Trench Mortar Battery. 5th June 1916 To 5th August 1916.		
War Diary	Albert	05/06/1916	26/07/1916
War Diary	St Ouen	29/07/1916	05/08/1916
Heading	8th, Division. Y/8, Medium T. M. Battery. September, 1916.		
Heading	Confidential. 8th Divisional Artillery. War Diary of Y/8 Medium Trench Mortar Bty. From 1-9-16 To 30.9.16. (Volume 1) With Appendices Nos. None		
War Diary	Hohenzollern Sector	01/09/1916	03/09/1916
War Diary	Gun G in Cromwell Rd.	03/09/1916	03/09/1916
War Diary	Gun F In Left Bayan	03/09/1916	03/09/1916
War Diary	Hohenzollern Sector	04/10/1916	04/10/1916
War Diary	E Gun Off Bart Alley (in OB1)	04/09/1916	04/09/1916
War Diary	F Gun In Left Bayan Gun Off Glamy Alley	04/09/1916	04/09/1916
War Diary	Hohenzollern Sector	06/09/1916	06/09/1916
War Diary	E Gun In OB1		
War Diary	Hohenzollern Sector	07/09/1916	09/09/1916
War Diary	E In OBI Off Battery Fin Left Bayan G In Cromwell Rd Off Quany Alley	09/09/1916	09/09/1916
War Diary	Hohenzollern Sector	10/09/1916	11/09/1916
War Diary	Hohenzollern Redoubt.	12/09/1916	12/09/1916
War Diary	Hohenzollern Sector	13/09/1916	13/09/1916
War Diary	Hohenzollern Redoubt	14/09/1916	14/09/1916
War Diary	Hohenzollern Sector	15/09/1916	28/09/1916
Heading	8th, Division. Y/8, Medium T.M. Battery. October, 1916.		
Heading	Confidential War Diary. Of Y/8 Medium Trench Mortar Battery From 1.10.16 To 31.10.16 Volume II		
War Diary	Hohenzollern Sector	01/10/1916	02/10/1916
War Diary	Hohenzollern Redoubt.	03/10/1916	31/10/1916
Heading	8th, Division. Y/8, Medium T. M. Battery. November, 1916.		
Heading	Confidential War Diary of Y/8 Medium Trench Mortar Battery From 1.11.16 To 30.11.16 Vol III		
War Diary	Citadel	01/11/1916	01/11/1916
War Diary	Postion A Mile NE Of Citadel	02/11/1916	06/11/1916
War Diary	Mansell Camp	07/11/1916	30/11/1916

Heading	8th, Division. Y/8, Medium T. M. Battery. December, 1916.		
Heading	Confidential War Diary of Y/8 Trench Mortar Battery From 1.12.16 To 31.12.16. Volume III		
War Diary	Line Of March	01/12/1916	01/12/1916
War Diary	Andainville (Somme)	02/12/1916	09/12/1916
War Diary	Liomer. (Somme)	10/12/1916	29/12/1916
Heading	8th, Division. Z/8, Medium T. M. Battery. September, 1916.		
Heading	Confidential 8th Divisional Artillery. War Diary Of Z/8 Medium Trench Mortar Bty. From 1-9-16 To 30.9.16. (Volume 1) With Appendices Nos. None		
War Diary	In The Fields	01/09/1916	30/09/1916
Heading	8th, Division. Z/8, Medium T. M. Battery. October, 1916.		
Heading	Confidential War Diary of Z/8 T. M. Battery From Oct 1 To Oct 31st 1916 Volume II		
War Diary	Puarmics Sector	01/10/1916	24/10/1916
Heading	8th, Division. Z/8 Medium T. M. Battery. November, 1916.		
Heading	Confidential War Diary Z/8 Trench Mortar Battery Period November 1st To 31st 1916 Vol III		
War Diary		01/11/1916	30/11/1916
Heading	8th, Division. Z/8, Medium T. M. Battery. December, 1916.		
Heading	Confidential War Diary Z/8 Trench Mortar Battery December 1st 1916 To December 31st 1916 Vol I		
War Diary		01/12/1916	31/12/1916
Heading	Confidential 8th Divisional Artillery War Diary of X-Y-Z Tw/8 T.M. Batteries From 1-1-17 To 31.1.17 (Volume 4)		
Heading	Confidential War Diary of X/8 Medium Trench Mortar Battery From 1-1-1917 To 31-1-17 Vol IV		
War Diary	In The Field	01/01/1917	31/01/1917
Heading	Confidential War Diary of Y/8 Medium Trench Mortar Battery From 1.1.17 To 31.1.17 Volume IV		
War Diary		01/01/1917	27/01/1917
Heading	Confidential War Diary of Z/8 Trench Mortar Battery From January 1st 1917 To January 31st 1917 Vol IV		
War Diary		01/01/1917	31/01/1917
Heading	Confidential War Diary W/8 Heavy Trench Mortar Battery From 1-1-1917 To 31-1-1917		
War Diary	Field	01/01/1917	31/01/1917
Heading	Confidential War Diary of Y/8 Medium Trench Mortar Battery From 1.1.17 To 31.1.17 Volume II		
War Diary		01/01/1917	27/01/1917
Heading	Confidential War Diary of X/8 T. M. Batt. From 1.1.1917 To 31.1.1917. Vol II		
War Diary	Court ?	01/01/1917	11/01/1917
War Diary	Vaux (Corbie)	12/01/1917	18/01/1917
War Diary	Vaux-L'amienois	19/01/1917	31/01/1917
Heading	Confidential 8th Divisional Artillery. War Diary of W.X.Y.Z. Trench Mortar Batteries From 1st Feby 1917 To 28 Feby 1917 (Volume VI)		
Heading	Confidential War Diary of W/8 Heavy Trench Mortar Battery From 1.2.17 To 28.2.17 Vol VI		

War Diary	In The Field	01/02/1917	28/02/1917
Heading	Confidential War Diary. Of X/8 Medium Trench Mortar Battery From 1.2.17 To 28.2.17 Vol VI		
War Diary	In The Field	01/02/1917	28/02/1917
Heading	Confidential War Diary Y/8 Medium Trench Mortar Battery From 1.2.17 To 28.2.17 Vol VI		
War Diary	In The Field	01/02/1917	28/02/1917
Heading	Confidential War Diary Z/8 Medium Trench Mortar Battery From 1.2.17 To 28.2.17 Vol VI		
War Diary	In The Field	01/02/1917	28/02/1917
Heading	Confidential. 8th Divisional Artillery. War Diary of W.X.Y.Z Trench Mortar Batteries From 1-3-17 To 31.3.17 (Volume VII) With Appendices Nos.		
Heading	Confidential. War Diary of X/8 Trench. Mortar Battery From 1-3-17 To 31-3-17 Vol 2.		
War Diary	Le-Forest	01/03/1917	03/03/1917
War Diary	S.W. Corner	04/03/1917	04/03/1917
War Diary	St. Purne Vassi Wood.	05/03/1917	25/03/1917
War Diary	Le Forest.	26/03/1917	31/03/1917
Heading	Secret War Diary of Y/8 Trench Mortar Battery From 1.III.17 To 31.III.17 Volume II		
War Diary	Near Bouchavesnes	04/03/1917	31/03/1917
Heading	Secret. War Diary of Z/8 Trench Mortar Battery. From 1 III 17 To 31 III 17 Volume II		
War Diary	Near Le Forest.	01/03/1917	31/03/1917
War Diary	In The Field	01/03/1917	31/03/1917
Heading	Confidential War Diary. W/8 Heavy Trench Mortar Battery. From 1-3-1917 To 31.3.1917 Vol II		
Heading	Confidential 8th Divisional Artillery. War Diary of W.X.Y.Z. Trench Mortar Batteries From 1.4.17 To 30.4.17. (Volume VII) With Appendices Nos		
War Diary	In The Field	01/04/1917	30/04/1917
War Diary	Haut-Allaines	01/04/1917	30/04/1917
War Diary	Le Forest	01/04/1917	23/04/1917
War Diary	Haut Allaines	24/04/1917	30/04/1917
War Diary	Haut-Allaines.	01/04/1917	25/04/1917
War Diary	Vaux-en-Amienois	26/04/1917	30/04/1917
Heading	Confidential 8th Divisional Artillery. War Diary Of W.X.Y.Z. Trench Mortar Batteries From 1-5-17 To 31.5.17. (Volume VIII) With Appendices Nos.		
Heading	Confidential War Diary of W/8 Heavy Trench Mortar Battery From 1.5.16 To 31.5.16 Vol VIII		
War Diary	Nurlu	01/05/1917	16/05/1917
War Diary	Dickebuche	17/05/1917	31/05/1917
Heading	Confidential War Diary of X/8 Trench Mortar Battery From 1-5-17 To 31-5-17 Vol VIII		
War Diary	Haut-Allaines	01/05/1917	15/05/1917
War Diary	Haut-Allaines	16/05/1917	20/05/1917
War Diary	Camp 112	21/05/1917	22/05/1917
War Diary	Arques	23/05/1917	24/05/1917
War Diary	Dickebush	25/05/1917	31/05/1917
Heading	War Diary of Y/8 Trench Mortar Battery From 1/5/17 To 31/5/17 Vol VIII		
War Diary	Haut-Allaines	01/05/1917	20/05/1917
War Diary	Camp 112	21/05/1917	22/05/1917
War Diary	Arques	23/05/1917	24/05/1917

War Diary	Dickebush	25/05/1917	31/05/1917
Heading	Confidential. War Diary of Z/8 T. M. Batt. From 1-5-17 To 31-5-17. (Volume VIII)		
War Diary	Vaux-En-Amienois.	01/05/1917	07/05/1917
War Diary	Nurlu	08/05/1917	14/05/1917
War Diary	Haut-Allaines	15/05/1917	24/05/1917
War Diary	Spoil Bank Sector (Ypres Salient)	25/05/1917	31/05/1917
Heading	Confidential 8th Divisional Artillery. War Diary of W.X.Y.Z. T. M. Batteries From 1st June To 30 June 1917 (Volume X) With Appendices Nos. 1		
Heading	Confidential War Diary of W/8 T.M. Batt. From 1-6-17 To 30-6-17. (Volume X) With Appendices.		
War Diary	Ypres	01/06/1917	11/06/1917
War Diary	Caistre	11/06/1917	14/06/1917
War Diary	Ypres Salient	14/06/1917	30/06/1917
Heading	Confidential War Diary X/8 Trench Mortar Battery From 1-6-17 To 30-6-17 Vol X		
War Diary	Hill 60	01/06/1917	07/06/1917
War Diary	Dickebush	08/06/1917	11/06/1917
War Diary	Caestre	12/06/1917	15/06/1917
War Diary	Ouderdom	16/06/1917	30/06/1917
Heading	Confidential War Diary Y/8 Trench Mortar Battery From 1.6.17 To 30.6.17 Volume X		
War Diary	Ypres Salient	01/06/1917	07/06/1917
War Diary	Ouderdom	07/06/1917	11/06/1917
War Diary	Caistre	11/06/1917	30/06/1917
Heading	War Diary of Z/8 Trench Mortar Battery From 1-6-17 To 30-6-17. Volume X		
War Diary	Ypres Salient	01/06/1917	11/06/1917
War Diary	Caestre	11/06/1917	11/06/1917
War Diary	Winnipeg Camp.	14/06/1917	14/06/1917
War Diary	North Of Ypres	16/06/1917	25/06/1917
Heading	Confidential 8th Divisional Artillery. War Diary of W.X.Y.Z. T.M. Batteries From 1st July To 30 July 1917 (Volume X) With Appendices Nos.		
Heading	Confidential War Diary of W/8 Trench Mortar Battery From 1-7-1917 To 30-7-1917 Vol II		
War Diary	East Of Ypres	01/07/1917	29/07/1917
Heading	Confidential War Diary X/8 Trench Mortar Battery From 1-7-16 To 31-7-17 Vol II		
War Diary		01/07/1917	31/07/1917
Heading	War Diary of Y/8 Trench Mortar Battery From 1/7/1917 To 31/7/1917 Vol II		
War Diary	Busse Boom	01/07/1917	29/07/1917
Heading	Confidential War Diary of Z/8 Trench Mortar Battery. From 1-7-1917 To 30-7-1917 Vol II		
War Diary	North Of Ypres	01/07/1917	29/07/1917
Heading	Confidential 8th Divisional Artillery. War Diary of W.X.Y.Z. T. M. Batteries From 31 7 To 31 8 17 (Volume II) With Appendices Nos		
War Diary	Ouderdom	01/08/1917	29/08/1917
War Diary	Caderdom	30/08/1917	31/08/1917
War Diary	Busse Boom	01/08/1917	29/08/1917
War Diary	Godewaersveldt.	30/08/1917	31/08/1917
War Diary	Busse Boom	01/08/1917	30/08/1917
War Diary	Godewearsvelde	31/08/1917	31/08/1917

War Diary	Ypres	01/08/1917	31/08/1917
Heading	Confidential War Diary X/8 Trench Mortar Battery From 1/9/17 To 30/9/17 Vol II		
War Diary	Godeswaervelde	01/09/1917	01/09/1917
War Diary	Baillual	02/09/1917	06/09/1917
War Diary	Neuve Eglise	07/09/1917	08/09/1917
War Diary	Nieppe	09/09/1917	30/09/1917
Heading	War Diary of Y/8 Trench Mortar Battery From 01/09/17 To 30/9/17 Vol II		
War Diary	Godewearsvelde.	01/09/1917	01/09/1917
War Diary	Balleul	02/09/1917	06/09/1917
War Diary	Neuve Eglise	06/09/1917	08/09/1917
War Diary	Nieppe	08/09/1917	30/09/1917
Heading	Confidential War Diary of Z/8 Trench Mortar Battery. From 01/09/17 To 30/09/17. Vol II		
War Diary	Godewaersveldt	01/09/1917	01/09/1917
War Diary	Bailleu	02/09/1917	06/09/1917
War Diary	Neuve Eglise	07/09/1917	08/09/1917
War Diary	Nieppe	09/09/1917	30/09/1917
Heading	Confidential War Diary W/8 Heavy. Trench. Mortar Bty. September Vol II		
War Diary	Godewaersveldt	01/09/1917	01/09/1917
War Diary	Bailleul	02/09/1917	06/09/1917
War Diary	Nieppe Eglise	07/09/1917	09/09/1917
War Diary	Nieppe	09/09/1917	30/09/1917
Heading	War-Diary Of X/8 Trench Mortar Battery From 1/10/17 To 31/10/17 Vol II		
War Diary	Nieppe	01/10/1917	31/10/1917
Heading	War Diary of Y/8 Trench Mortar Bty From 1/10/17 To 31/10/17 Vol II		
War Diary	Nieppe	01/10/1917	31/10/1917
Heading	Confidential War Diary of Z/8 Trench Mortar Battery From 1/10/17 To 31/10/17 Vol II		
War Diary	Nieppe	01/10/1917	31/10/1917
Heading	Confidential War Diary of X/8 Heavy Trench Motar Battery From 1-10-17 To Vol II		
War Diary	Ploegsteert	01/10/1917	31/10/1917
Heading	H.Q.R.A. 8 Div Therewith War Diaries Of 8 Div T M Bts For The Month Of November		
Heading	War Diary of X/8 Trench Mortar Battery From 1/11/17 To 30/11/17 Vol II		
War Diary	Neippe	01/11/1917	09/11/1917
War Diary	New Area	10/11/1917	30/11/1917
Miscellaneous	8th Divisional Artillery. Casualties That Have Occurred In Personnel During Month Ending November 1917		
Heading	War Diary of Y/8 Trench Mortar Bty. From 1-11-17 To 30-11-17 Vol II		
War Diary	Nieppe	01/11/1917	10/11/1917
War Diary	Krustraat Erea	11/11/1917	30/11/1917
Miscellaneous	8th Divisional Artillery, Casualties That Have Occurred In Personnel During Month Ending November		
Heading	Confidential War Diary of Z/8 Trench Mortar Bty From 1-11-17 To 30-11-17 Vol II		
War Diary	Nieppe	01/11/1917	10/11/1917
War Diary	Krusstraat Area	11/11/1917	30/11/1917

Miscellaneous	8th Divisional Artillery. Casualties That Have Occurred In Personnel During Month Ending 30th November.	30/11/1917	30/11/1917
Heading	Confidential War Diary of W/8 Heavy Trench Mortar Battery From 1-11-17 To 30-11-17 Vol II		
War Diary		01/11/1917	30/11/1917
Miscellaneous	8th Divisional Artillery. Casualties That Have Occurred In Personnel During Month Ending November.		
Heading	War-Diary Of X/8 Trench Mortar Battery R.A. From 1-12-17 To 31-12-17 Vol II		
War Diary	Kaaustraat Area H.16.5.20	01/12/1917	09/12/1917
War Diary	Hamentings	10/12/1917	31/12/1917
Miscellaneous	8th Divisional Artillery. Casualties That Have Occurred In Personnel During Month Ending December 197.		
Heading	War Diary of Y/8 Trench Mortar Bty From 1-12-1917 To 31-12-17 Vol II		
War Diary	Krustraat	01/12/1917	09/12/1917
War Diary	Vlamertinghe	10/12/1917	31/12/1917
Miscellaneous	8th Divisional Artillery. Casualties That Have Occurred In Personnel During Month Ending December 1917		
Heading	Confidential War Diary of Z/8 Trench Mortar Battery. From 1-12-17 To 31-12-17 Vol II		
War Diary	Krusstraat Area	01/12/1917	09/12/1917
War Diary	Vlamertinghe	10/12/1917	31/12/1917
Miscellaneous	8th Divisional Artillery. Casualties That Have Occurred In Personnel During Month Ending 31st Dec In Z/8 T.M. Bty	31/12/1917	31/12/1917
Heading	Confidential War Diary of W/8 Trench Mortar Battery From 1-12-17 To 31-12-17. 1917 Vol II		
War Diary		01/12/1917	31/12/1917
Miscellaneous	8th Divisional Artillery. Casualties That Have Occurred In Personnel During Month Ending December 31-12-17.	31/12/1917	31/12/1917
Miscellaneous	8th Divisional Artillery. Casualties That Have Occurred In Personnel During Month Ending		
Heading	War Diary of Y/8 Trench Mortar Bty From 1-1-1918 To 31-1-1918. Vol III		
War Diary	Vlamertinghe	01/01/1918	21/01/1918
War Diary	Poperinghe	22/01/1918	31/01/1918
Miscellaneous	8th Divisional Artillery. Casualties That Have Occurred In Personnel During Month Ending January 1918.		
Heading	Confidential War Diary of Z/8 Trench Mortar Bty 1-1-18 To 31-1-18. Vol III		
War Diary	Flamertinghe	01/01/1918	20/01/1918
War Diary	Poperinghe	21/01/1918	31/01/1918
Miscellaneous	8th Divisional Artillery. Casualties That Have Occurred In Personnel During Month Ending 31st January	31/01/1918	31/01/1918
Heading	War-Diary Of X/8 Trench Mortar Battery R.A. From 1-1-18 To 31-1-18 Vol III		
War Diary	Flamentinge	01/01/1918	21/01/1918
War Diary	Poperinghe	22/01/1918	31/01/1918
Miscellaneous	8th Divisional Artillery. Casualties That Have Occurred In Personnel During Month Ending January 1918.		
Heading	Confidential War Diary of W/8 Heavy. Trench. Mortar. Bty From 1-1-18 To 31-1-18 Vol III		
War Diary		09/01/1918	31/01/1918
Heading	To Brigade Major R A 8th Div Arty		

Type	Location	From	To
War Diary	In The Field	01/02/1918	28/02/1918
War Diary	In The Field	17/02/1918	28/02/1918
War Diary	In The Field	01/02/1918	16/02/1918
Heading	War Diary 8th Divisional Trench Mortar Batteries, R.A. March 1918		
War Diary	In The Field	01/03/1918	31/03/1918
Miscellaneous	Appendix		
Heading	8th Divisional Artillery. 8th Divisional Trench Mortar Officer April 1918.		
Miscellaneous	To Staff Capt R.A. 8th Div Arty	30/04/1918	30/04/1918
War Diary	In The Field	01/04/1918	30/04/1918
War Diary	Bray Les Mareille	01/05/1918	13/05/1918
War Diary	Roucy	13/05/1918	18/05/1918
War Diary	Laplat Rerie	19/05/1918	30/05/1918
War Diary	Marne District	01/06/1918	18/06/1918
War Diary	Dourier Nr Airaimes	18/06/1918	23/06/1918
War Diary	Embre Ville	24/06/1918	30/06/1918
War Diary	Embermille	01/07/1918	17/07/1918
War Diary	Curtore	19/07/1918	21/07/1918
War Diary	Vimy	22/07/1918	31/07/1918
War Diary	Caestre	01/08/1918	28/08/1918
War Diary	Vimy	29/08/1918	31/08/1918
Heading	War Diary August 1918 8th Div. T.M. Bde.		
War Diary	Oppy	01/09/1918	30/09/1918
War Diary	Oppy	01/10/1918	11/10/1918
War Diary	Roolincourt	12/10/1918	12/10/1918
War Diary	Fampoux	13/10/1918	13/10/1918
War Diary	Fresnes	15/10/1918	19/10/1918
War Diary	Planque	20/10/1918	21/10/1918
War Diary	Cattelet	22/10/1918	25/10/1918
War Diary	Ponchelet	26/10/1918	30/10/1918
War Diary	Millon Fosse	31/10/1918	31/10/1918

$$\frac{1696}{3} \quad \frac{code \; es}{}$$

1.30

1 hour 40 min

8TH DIVISION

TRENCH MORTAR BATTERIES

MAY 1916 - OCT 1918

8th Div.
I.Corps.

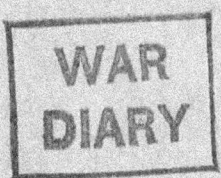

M/8 TRENCH MORTAR BATTERY.

25th May 1916 to 8th August 1916.

Oct 1918

WAR DIARY 30.10.16
INTELLIGENCE SUMMARY

To Officer i/c Records
A.G.'s Office.
Base.

Sir,

Herewith
War diary of M/8 T.M.B.
from May 25th 1916 to
Aug 8th 1916

C. Ellis 2Lt RFA
O.C. Y/8 TMB

Army Form C. 2118.

Instructions regarding War Diaries and Intelligence Summaries are contained in F. S. Regs., Part II. and the Staff Manual respectively. Title Pages will be prepared in manuscript.

(Erase heading not required.)

Confidential

WAR DIARY of M 8 or U 8 Trench Mortar Battery Y.

FROM MAY 25th/6 — To Aug. 8th 1916

France.

Formed 5th June 1916
Disbanded 8th August 1916

Place	Date	Hour	Summary of Events and Information	Remarks and references to Appendices

M.G. Trench Mortar Battery.
A Supernumerary Battery for Somme Offensive. **WAR DIARY**
or
INTELLIGENCE SUMMARY.
(Erase heading not required.)

Year 1916.

Army Form C. 2118.

Instructions regarding War Diaries and Intelligence Summaries are contained in F. S. Regs., Part II. and the Staff Manual respectively. Title pages will be prepared in manuscript.

Place	Date	Hour	Summary of Events and Information	Remarks and references to Appendices
ALBERT.	May 25th	—	Personel of Battery arrived. There were no officer Lieut T.A. TRUMAN R.F.A. and 23 other ranks drawn from Units of 8th Division Artillery. Billets were taken up in RUE DE BAPAUME, ALBERT.	
"	26th		Personel were sent off to schools for instruction in Artillery 4 gun pits, There were Y.S.3 position 127 N.F. BACON R.F.A. joined Battery	
"	27th		Position was reconnoitred for a battery position and suitable area near junction of THORESBY ST. and LONGRIDGE ST. and shafts for entrance to Pits started. Tunnelling 5' x 10' x 6'.	
	June 1st 3rd 5th		Whole Battery with 4 guns borrowed from Y.S. T.M. By left at 10 am in 3 motor omnibuses for 4th Army School of Mortars at VALHEUREUX.	
	6th		Weeks course started. Drill for mixing and mounting and chamonite guns was taught. Firing rounds and first fired and then 15 live rounds. Course finished. 4 guns arrived at ALBERT. for M.G.	

M.G. Trench Mortar Battery
a Summary Battery for Somme Offensive.

WAR DIARY or INTELLIGENCE SUMMARY.

Army Form C. 2118.

Year 1916.

Place	Date	Hour	Summary of Events and Information	Remarks and references to Appendices
ALBERT.	June 12th-14th		Battery returned to ALBERT. Started digging good positions near THE NAB, near AUTHUILLE WOOD. It was now said that "situation was becoming desperate" so work was carried on night and day with the utmost energy and labor available.	
	16th		It was decided to have 1,30 rounds per mortar, no reserves to get this huge amount of ammunition up to the guns it was necessary to use as far as we carried of the wood in wagons G.S. and then carried by infantry fatigue parties from there to the guns. This was done by night over the top and by day along communication trenches. Infantry carrying party 50 strong reported BONISTON POST 9-15 p.m. and carried up 300 bombs empltie. This was party carried up trenches and then remainder after dark was taken over the top.	
	18th		Many 240 bombs were carried up trenches by day with great exertion & caution	

M.S. Trench Mortar Battery.
A Supplementary Battery 4th Somme Offensive. WAR DIARY

Army Form C. 2118.

INTELLIGENCE SUMMARY.

Year 1916

Place	Date	Hour	Summary of Events and Information	Remarks and references to Appendices
ALBERT.	24th		The 6th the guns were not firing but were gradually turned by chalk, and trouble with Light mechanism before. We then ceased firing at 8 a.m. and commenced to tidy jet up a little, then returned to billets.	
"	25th night		We dug out No 4th pit and No 3 and prepared for next day's shoot.	
"	25th	4 am to 8 am 3-30 pm to 4 pm 6.0 pm to 7-30 pm.	Battery started firing 5 am and went on till 8 am when trouble began with night mechanism and pit fell in. Enemy shelling by enemy not severe.	
"	26th		We moved out of billets in HEBERT into some fields near town.	
"	27th	6 am to 10 am 4-30 pm to 30 pm.	Fired with 3 guns in action and fire was never observed from Quarter of QUARRY BRAE and front line trench. No 1 gun used 7 rifles when mechanism went.	

Army Form C. 2118.

M. & . Trench Mortar Battery.
A Supplementary Battery for the Somme Offensive

WAR DIARY
or
INTELLIGENCE SUMMARY.
(Erase heading not required.)

Year 1916

Instructions regarding War Diaries and Intelligence Summaries are contained in F. S. Regs., Part II. and the Staff Manual respectively. Title pages will be prepared in manuscript.

Place	Date	Hour	Summary of Events and Information	Remarks and references to Appendices
ALBERT.	June 19th	night	400 trench complete were carried up to position.	
"	21st	day	240 bombs complete were carried up trenches very exhausting.	
"	21st	night	Four guns complete were taken from billets & tags C.S.S. up to head quarters and then carried in to position.	
"	22nd		Two beds were dug in carefully with "K" Any Entrenchments.	
"	23rd		Remaining two beds wrought to position.	
"	24th		Commencement of Bombardment. Same effect of Artillery was kept all over to a width of about 300 yards and a depth of 30 yards. The bombard much by good shrapnel de fire. "B" Battery opened fire at 4.30 and on to some. Our artillery support was very feeble. About 8"am German 5-9" Battery announced our fire vigorously with it's search staff. A direct hit was obtained at it's observation. B.K. LONGRIDGE S.I. standing No. 94 strangely good a hiera- in a little while after. No. 94 strangely good a hiera- in the pit wounding B. J. Scott and knocking pit all in	

M 9 Trench Mortar Battery

A Summary Battery for the Somme Offensive

WAR DIARY or **INTELLIGENCE SUMMARY**
(Erase heading not required.)

Army Form C. 2118.

Instructions regarding War Diaries and Intelligence Summaries are contained in F. S. Regs., Part II. and the Staff Manual respectively. Title pages will be prepared in manuscript.

Year 1916.

Place	Date	Hour	Summary of Events and Information	Remarks and references to Appendices
ALBERT.	28th		4 am to 6 am, 7.30 am to 8.30 and 2 pm to 4 pm Fired with 3 guns in relays as No 4 pit was unsafe, obtained rifle meteorogram until guns troubles, and used heavy shell fire on whole shelling in rides of No 1 Pit. Assault was now postponed 48 hrs so we commenced to bombard enemy front line with delay action (bridges).	
"	29th		4 am to 6 am, 7.30 am to 8.30 am, 2 pm to 4 pm Fired, No 2 gun completely blown in flow putting gun temporarily out of action.	
"	30th		4 am to 6.30 am, 7.30 am to 8.30 am to 6.30 am 2 pm to 4 pm. Shelled by heavy artillery and "overly heavy loss" mainly, Col Thomas in the s. fore arm.	
"	July 1st		Morning of Assault by 8th Division 7-30 am. Battery fired on enemy front line with 3 guns 6-25 am to 7-29 am. 32 rounds in all. This went well although on 4 Battery did 97 rounds in all, the 2nd Bttn Lincolns attacking in our front. under heavy shell fire.	

M.S. Trench Mortar Battery

Army Form C. 2118.

WAR DIARY or INTELLIGENCE SUMMARY.
(Erase heading not required.)

Year 1916.

Place	Date	Hour	Summary of Events and Information	Remarks and references to Appendices
ALBERT	July 1st		Attack and how after several reports were sent left, no infantry seen & gun longbit . Other guns left this time, forage & brass was very heavy. The following casualties received the day. Killed Gr Cumberworth, Rumcle, Gr Mahe, Gr Byer, Gr Tridge, Gr Dugdale, Gr Childs, Gr Cumants, Gr Forts, McCulke. As it was now evident we could not take our guns forward as originally intended, limited till midday & lifted wounded men away, and proceeded taking place of litter bearers. At midday were moved down to CHERRY Ree, where help was given to clearing station , we were retired to "Billets" all night, rank very tired.	
"	2nd		Back at Billets resting.	
"	3rd		12th Division now went to attack no Battery was ordered to bombard enemy trenches, 2 Guns bombarded from 2-15 am to 3-15 am and again to	

T2131. W⋅⋅W⋅⋅ 4/15. Grd J.C. & S. 3-15 am.

Army Form C. 2118.

176 Trench Mortar Battery
A Summary Battery for the Somme Offensive WAR DIARY
or
INTELLIGENCE SUMMARY
(Erase heading not required.)

Year 1916.

Instructions regarding War Diaries and Intelligence
Summaries are contained in F. S. Regs., Part II.
and the Staff Manual respectively. Title pages
will be prepared in manuscript.

Place	Date	Hour	Summary of Events and Information	Remarks and references to Appendices
ALBERT.	July. 3rd		Our flanks were plainly visible as it was dawn with the result that the enemy fire in us was terrific. We suffered no casualties of this period.	
			How Purnell then relieved Swany Brae & was forced into we were subjected to shrapnel and pretty nasty shell fire. Collman was two wounded. by a piece of shell near BLIGHTY VILLA in crossing 8 Return.	
	4th & 5th	Night	Our whole of equipment was withdrawn from the line, an inspection of this, all were absolutely plastered in by enemy shell fire.	
	19th	12 mid. night	Left ALBERT. STN. by train for railhead of 8th Div. arrived at BETHUNE & is there billeted near station.	
BETHUNE	22nd			
	24th Aug. 8th		Left Bethune for SAILLY LABOURSE. N.C.O's of Battery were relieved of their units the arrangements being transferred to H.S.T.M.B.	

M.8. Trench Mortar Battery
A Summary Battery for the Somme offensive WAR DIARY
Year 1916.
Army Form C. 2118.
INTELLIGENCE SUMMARY.

Place	Date	Hour	Summary of Events and Information	Remarks and references to Appendices
In the Field	Aug 8th		M.8. Trench Mortar Battery was first called V.8. It was formed on June 5th based on a nucleus and fired in a bombardment and was out of action till all written a month.	
	16		2 officers were detached from "O" Battery R.H.A. and its ranks drawn from different units of Divisional Artillery. All recruits had only 10 weeks training as Trench Mortars as at the first normal fired in the line was found at the commencement of the bombardment 24th June.	

Tom Roberts
Lt R.H.A.
8/8/16.

Cmdg M.8. T.M. By.
1/1/16.

8th, Division.

V?W.X.Y.Z. T. M. Battery.

August, 1916.

CONFIDENTIAL.

8th DIVISIONAL ARTILLERY.

WAR DIARY

OF

V, W, X, Y, Z, T.M. Batteries

From 1-8-16 To 31-8-16

(VOLUME 1)

With APPENDICES Nos. None

Army Form C. 2118.

X/8, Y/8 and Z/8(M) Trench Mortar Batteries.
WAR DIARY
or
INTELLIGENCE SUMMARY.
(Erase heading not required.)

Instructions regarding War Diaries and Intelligence Summaries are contained in F. S. Regs., Part II. and the Staff Manual respectively. Title pages will be prepared in manuscript.

VOL I

Place	Date	Hour	Summary of Events and Information	Remarks and references to Appendices
SAILLY LA BOURSE	1.8.16	—	Rifle Grenade Bombardment carried out by Lt. T.M. Batteries in conjunction with 18 Pdr and 4.5" How. Batteries. Attempts fired. Retaliation slight.	
	2.8.16	—	Enemy mortars fairly active and in retaliation opened on QUARRY. Y/8 T.M. Battery replied by a rifle grenade Gun fire chiefly in nature of retaliation - Rounds 300 - 300	
	3.8.16	—	Relief of Z/R T.M. Battery moves to Quarries. Relief from Crinchly Posts.	
	4.8.16	—		
	5.8.16	—	Enemy much activity from our own and enemy mortars to their rotting of intention to renew	
	6.8.16	—		
	7.8.16	—	Enemy activity on both sides	
	8.8.16	—	Enemy retired and to repairing wire	
	9.8.16	—	Enemy fired in retaliation, also fired shortly on our own front line trenches.	
	10.8.16	—	Nothing of interest to record	

Army Form C. 2118.

X/8, Y/8 and 2/8(M) Trench Mortar Batteries.

WAR DIARY
or
INTELLIGENCE SUMMARY.
(Erase heading not required.)

Instructions regarding War Diaries and Intelligence Summaries are contained in F.S. Regs., Part II. and the Staff Manual respectively. Title pages will be prepared in manuscript.

Place	Date	Hour	Summary of Events and Information	Remarks and references to Appendices
SAILLY LA BOURSE	12.8.16		Some fire shortly was down on enemy as Kitchener Cuv Roads	
	13.8.16		also on MM on upon Brigade front. Nothing of importance to report	
	14.8.16 15.8.16 16.8.16		Rather but normal activity on both sides	
	17.8.16		Around activity. Enemy Heavy Emplacement on left of Duck were successfully engaged by our artillery	
	18.8.16 19.8.16 20.8.16		Listening of enemy trenches	
	21.8.16		Can not report any activity in offensive trenches again in retaliation. Rather quiet	
	22.8.16 23.8.16 24.8.16 25.8.16 26.8.16		Around activity. Columns of our enemy were seen moving	
	27.8.16 28.8.16		Normal	

Army Form C. 2118.

X/8, Y/8 and 2/8 Trench Mortar Batteries.
(M)

WAR DIARY
or
INTELLIGENCE SUMMARY.

(Erase heading not required.)

Instructions regarding War Diaries and Intelligence Summaries are contained in F. S. Regs., Part II. and the Staff Manual respectively. Title pages will be prepared in manuscript.

Place	Date	Hour	Summary of Events and Information	Remarks and references to Appendices
SAILLY LA BOURSE	29.8.16		Two combined schemes carried out in HOHENZOLLERN and HULLUCH Sections. Good results.	
	30.8.16			
	31.8.16		Settling of information to men.	
	1.9.16			H.Gwaters Capt D.T.M.O. 8th Div R.A. X/8, Y/8 and 2/8 T.M. Batteries for O.C.

Army Form C. 2118.

V/8(H) Trench Mortar Battery
WAR DIARY
INTELLIGENCE SUMMARY

(Erase heading not required.)

Place	Date	Hour	Summary of Events and Information	Remarks and references to Appendices
SAILLY LA BOURSE	1.8.16 to 31.8.16		This battery has been kept in readiness in emplacements and for the one gun so far in charge. Only action for the past time on 25.8.16 firing eleven rounds. Emplacements and dugouts to be kept in working order. Training continues.	

E.G. Walker
Capt
O.T.M.O.
for O.C. V/8 Heavy T.M. Battery

1.9.16

Army Form C. 2118.

W/8 (H) Trench Mortar Battery.

WAR DIARY
or
INTELLIGENCE SUMMARY.
(Erase heading not required.)

Instructions regarding War Diaries and Intelligence Summaries are contained in F.S. Regs., Part II. and the Staff Manual respectively. Title pages will be prepared in manuscript.

Place	Date	Hour	Summary of Events and Information	Remarks and references to Appendices
SAILLY LA BOURSE	1.8.16 6 3.8.16		Since coming to the Somme Douai, the Battery has not been in action. The Battery being employed in fatigues for the Heavy T.M. Batteries and the other Heavy Batteries of the Division. There is therefore nothing of interest to record. L. Groome Capt. D.S.M.O. for O.C. W/8 Heavy T.M. Battery 1.8.16.	

8th, Division.

W/8, Heavy T. M. Battery.

September, 1916.

CONFIDENTIAL.

8th DIVISIONAL ARTILLERY.

WAR DIARY

OF

W/8. Heavy T.M. Battery

From 1-9-16 To 30-9-16

(VOLUME 4)

With APPENDICES Nos. One

Vol 4

Army Form C. 2118.

WAR DIARY
or
INTELLIGENCE SUMMARY
(Erase heading not required.)

W/8 Heavy Trench Mortar Battery.

September 1916.

Army Form C. 2118.

WAR DIARY
INTELLIGENCE SUMMARY
(Erase heading not required.)

Instructions regarding War Diaries and Intelligence Summaries are contained in F. S. Regs., Part II. and the Staff Manual respectively. Title Pages will be prepared in manuscript.

Place	Date	Hour	Summary of Events and Information	Remarks and references to Appendices
SAILLY	1.9.16		The following has been out of action where there has been	
LA BOURSE	21.9.16		no matter. The personnel has been employed on fatigues for the stay behind as the Division, as there is nothing of interest to record.	Reg
	22.9.16		Rocca taken over from 3rd Divn in Howitzer Park was 50 rounds of ammunition	Reg
	24.9.16		Few repaired rounds fired with satisfactory result.	Reg
	29.9.16		A convoy party of 5. from the howitzer of this battery were ordered this rail on arrival about being on guard and ammunition b	Reg for change T
	30.9.16		Rocking of influence to record.	Reg

L.C. Walsh
Capt.
O.T.M.O. P.S. 2nd R.A.

Army Form C. 2118.

WAR DIARY
or
INTELLIGENCE SUMMARY
(Erase heading not required.) Appendix I

Instructions regarding War Diaries and Intelligence Summaries are contained in F. S. Regs., Part II and the Staff Manual respectively. Title Pages will be prepared in manuscript.

Place	Date	Hour	Summary of Events and Information	Remarks and references to Appendices
	29.9.16		The following were the casualties referred to G.1:—	
			Bdr. 81160 Gunner Beecham A Killed	
			„ 35458 „ Hyre G Wounded	
			„ 33310 „ Holeroyd R „	
			„ 15874 „ Goering J „	
			„ 23573 „ Tyer a „	
			LEdwards Capt	
			D.T.M.O.P.S 24th D.A.	

8th, Division.

W/8, Heavy T. M. Battery.

October, 1916.

Army Form C. 2118.

WAR DIARY
or
INTELLIGENCE SUMMARY.
(Erase heading not required.)

Confidential

War Diary
W/8 Heavy Trench Mortar Battery.
From 1.10.16. — 31.10.16.
Vol. II

Army Form C. 2118.

WAR DIARY
or
INTELLIGENCE SUMMARY.
(Erase heading not required.)

Instructions regarding War Diaries and Intelligence Summaries are contained in F. S. Regs., Part II. and the Staff Manual respectively. Title pages will be prepared in manuscript.

Place	Date	Hour	Summary of Events and Information	Remarks and references to Appendices
Fallasfeld	1/9/16		From 1-10-16 till the 16-10-16. This Battery had one gun in the Shulluch sector. But it only fired 5 rounds as the position was a very bad one. It was taken over from the 3 Division. Lt. Morris had charge of the gun together with a Medium Battery. The remainder of the Bty was on fatigues.	
	16/10/16		On the 16th 10-16 the Bty took over two guns in the Carnoïn Sector given by the 32 Division.	T.A.M.
	17/10		15 Rounds were fired. Two rounds fell short. But just two had been dams	T.A.M.
	18/10		20 Rounds were fired with excellent results	T.A.M.
	19/10		16 Rounds were fired in retaliation to enemy fire which was very heavy.	T.A.M.
	20/10		13 Rounds were fired in conjunction with Medium & Heavy Artillery, results were very good	T.A.M.
	21/10		A Gun was out of action owing to the rod giving way. It was put in ready by the 32 div	
	21/9/16		The guns were handed over 15 y/21. The detachments were withdrawn the same evening to their billets 7/21 in Sailly La Bourse.	T.B.M. T.A.M.
	22/9/16		Lt Morris took over W/R Battery.	

Army Form C. 2118.

WAR DIARY
or
INTELLIGENCE SUMMARY.
(Erase heading not required.)

Place	Date	Hour	Summary of Events and Information	Remarks and references to Appendices
Fultsfield	22.10.16.		The Battery left Sailly-La-Bourse for the Somme. They proceeded by Lorries	
	23.10.16.		to Bethune where they spent the night.	
	24.-		Bty entrained	
	25.-		Still on train	
	26.-		" " "	
	27.-		" " "	
	28.-		Bty detrained at Edgehill [struck] in the midnight 27/28 to 10 and marched to the Citadel arriving at 3 A.M. & spent the day humping kit up	
	29.10.16.		Nil	
	30.10.16		5 men N.C.O. departed on fatigues to Guillemont Station	
	31.10.16			

F.G. Mitchell 2/L: R.O.
J.W. Cowdry W/8 HTM (31.10.16)

8th, Division.

W/8, Heavy T. M. Battery.

November, 1916.

Army Form C. 2118.

WAR DIARY
or
INTELLIGENCE SUMMARY.
(Erase heading not required.)

Confidential
War Diary
of
M/8 Heavy Trench Mortar Battery
from 24th 11/16 - - - 30/4/16

Volume III

WAR DIARY
or
INTELLIGENCE SUMMARY

Army Form C. 2118.

Place	Date	Hour	Summary of Events and Information	Remarks and references to Appendices
In the Field	27/11/16		General fatigue under orders of the Division.	
	28/11/16		" " "	
	29/11/16 to 30/11/16		Line of march.	

P. Munro Lieut R.F.A
I Comdg A/8 T.M.Batty

8th, Division.

W/8, Heavy T. M. Battery.

December, 1916.

Army Form C. 2118.

WAR DIARY
or
INTELLIGENCE SUMMARY.
(Erase heading not required.)

Confidential

War Diary

W/18 Heavy Trench Mortar Battery

From 1st 12.16 —————— to 31.12.16

Vol III

G Muir / Capt
O Comdg /W/18 Hy T M B

Army Form C. 2118.

WAR DIARY
or
INTELLIGENCE SUMMARY.
(Erase heading not required.)

Instructions regarding War Diaries and Intelligence Summaries are contained in F. S. Regs., Part II. and the Staff Manual respectively. Title pages will be prepared in manuscript.

Place	Date	Hour	Summary of Events and Information	Remarks and references to Appendices
In Field	1/12/15 to 2/12/15		Line of march	—
	3/12/15 to 29/12/15		In rest & training	—
	29/12/15 to 31/12/15		Line of march	—

8th, Division.

X/8, Medium T. M. Battery.

September, 1916.

CONFIDENTIAL.

8th DIVISIONAL ARTILLERY.

WAR DIARY

OF

X/8. Medium Trench Mortar Bty

From 1-9-16 To 30-9-16

(VOLUME 1.)

With APPENDICES Nos. None.

Army Form C. 2118.

WAR DIARY
or
INTELLIGENCE SUMMARY
(Erase heading not required.)

Instructions regarding War Diaries and Intelligence Summaries are contained in F. S. Regs., Part II. and the Staff Manual respectively. Title Pages will be prepared in manuscript.

Place	Date	Hour	Summary of Events and Information	Remarks and references to Appendices
Vermelles	14/7/1915		During the first eleven days of the month no events of tactical interest went over kept, so that general results are embodied in the following résumé. Ammunition Expenditure. During the 2.1 days from the 9/6 to 2.9/6 we fired a daily average of 48.14 rounds per gun in action. It is estimated that during the month the average number of gun in action at one time was six. The current state of affairs in summarised for by the following:– Rifle Mechanisms. We have had constant trouble from rifle mechanisms becoming cracked, the mixture being far too light to stand the shock of discharge of the gun. In spite of the utmost care in seeing that the mechanisms were slightly screwed into the gun they have been constantly thrown out, in some cases the mechanism being shattered, & in others the gun threads on the gun or adapter worn torn, necessitating	L.M.G gun ... L.M.G gun

Army Form C. 2118.

WAR DIARY
or
INTELLIGENCE SUMMARY

(Erase heading not required.)

X/8 Medium Trench Mortar Battery

Summary of Events & Information

for the month ending September 30th. 1916.

WAR DIARY
or
INTELLIGENCE SUMMARY

Army Form C. 2118.

(Erase heading not required.)

2.

The gun being sent to ordnance, completely out of action.

Militaria. Hostile reply to our fire up to Sept 27th (approx) has been heavy & on the whole accurate. Our employment was more or less slow. On one of these Sept 26th the gun part temperament out of action & 9 occasions. On one of these Sept 26th the gun frame & rifle mechanism were very badly damaged. On this last occasion it was thought it a shell - a most of the other occasions the damage was done by maneuvering which out ranges us.

Observation. The enemy in this respect has the advantage. If the Si observed by or reported to us.

Observation of the Division the mounts or have been issued with a No 14. Periscope. This instrument is of the greatest value in this work.

E Cunningham

3.

Ammunition has been much more reliable than it was during August. There have been fewer "duds" & the charges have been noticeably better, there having been practically no rounds falling dangerously short.

General Firing Results. In numerous engagements against small targets, such as M.G. Emplacements, snipers' Posts etc., the 2" M.T.M. is to emit. the range for elevation can rarely be relied upon closer than 50 ft to 100 yards & in regard to line it is a common happening for the gun to alter 3 or 4 degrees for no known reason.

On Sept 24th the Battery moved from Cellar in Vermelles to home billets at Noyelles. The men are greatly appreciating the change.

Ernest V Thompson
OC X/8 TMB

30/9/16

8th, Division.

X/8, T. M. Battery.

October, 1916.

Army Form C. 2118.

WAR DIARY
or
INTELLIGENCE SUMMARY.
(Erase heading not required.)

CONFIDENTIAL
WAR DIARY
OF
X/8 T.M.B.

From Oct 1st 1916
to
Oct 31st 1916

Volume II

Signed OC X/8 T.M.B.

Army Form C. 2118.

WAR DIARY
or
INTELLIGENCE SUMMARY.
(Erase heading not required.)

No of Reserves

Place	Date	Hour	Summary of Events and Information	Remarks and references to Appendices
Hohenzollern REDOUBT and Right	1/10/16		Enemy very quiet	34
"	2		Engaged M.G. emplacement in G.5.C.5.2. Several hits obtained. Operation offensive	55
"	3		Fired on enemy front line in G.5.C.5. Enemy quiet. Operation offensive	52
"	4		Fired on wire & observed good results G.5.C.S.75.25. & G.5.C.5.2. Opportunity	59
"	5		Fired during night in conjunction with Arty + M.G. + L.T.M. all night S.O.S. S.O.S.	150
"	6		Enemy very quiet. Breached parapet at G.5.C.5.2. Enfiladed enemy's known Reptenbrachofen all night. Sniper obtained a good bag of 46 mm. S/F Off	19
"	7			20
"	8		Fired on trench. Gun Sniper still active. Operation offensive	39
"	9		Communication trenches kept under heavy fire. Operation offensive	43
"	10		Shelled G.5.C.5.2. Great damage. Retaliation enemy's Arty. Opportunity & Obs	74
"	11		Rifle medium in B. Gun out of action, otherwise as on 11th. Defensive	78
"	12		Kept on Clifford Craters &c Conjunction Dithers	64
"	13		Premature burst in B Gun. Corporal Gawne killed & Pmt Bent wounded	81
"	14		Clifford Crater & G.5.C.52. Subjected to heavy bombardment. Offensive Offensive	89
"	15		Breach in parapet at G.5.C.53. Repaired	106
"	16		Shelled G.11.C. and all approaches	64

Army Form C. 2118.

WAR DIARY
or
INTELLIGENCE SUMMARY.
(Erase heading not required.)

Instructions regarding War Diaries and Intelligence Summaries are contained in F. S. Regs., Part II. and the Staff Manual respectively. Title pages will be prepared in manuscript.

Place	Date	Hour	Summary of Events and Information	Remarks and references to Appendices
Hohenzollern Redoubt & Right	Sept 1916 17		Fired on Q.5.c.6.3. Much timber observed thrown up — Coy. Stokes	67
	18		Steady fire kept on enemy trenches on our front — Offensive	66
	19		Engaged G.5. 8.5.2 in attempt to derive damage — Defensive	91
	20th		Enemy wire cut & Communication trenches shelled.	39
	21st		Reverted to defensive ops owing to shortage of Rifle Mechanism.	40
	22nd		Same as 21st	38
	22nd to 31st		Nothing to note in action — withdrawn from line. Average number of guns in action from 1st/9/16 — 22/9/16 was 2. Average number of rounds fired from 1st/9/16 — 22/9/16 was 65.9	

Signed Ernest S. Morgan 2/Lieut R.F.A.
O.C. 2 x/8 T.M.B

8th, Division.

X/8, T. M. Battery.

November, 1916.

Army Form C. 2118.

WAR DIARY
or
INTELLIGENCE SUMMARY.
(Erase heading not required.)

Confidential

War Diary of X/8 T.M.B.
from 1st/12/16.
31st/10/16 to 1st/12/16.

Vol. III

Army Form C. 2118.

WAR DIARY
or
INTELLIGENCE SUMMARY.
(Erase heading not required.)

Instructions regarding War Diaries and Intelligence Summaries are contained in F. S. Regs., Part II. and the Staff Manual respectively. Title pages will be prepared in manuscript.

Place	Date	Hour	Summary of Events and Information	Remarks and references to Appendices
Moascar Camp Egypt	1st/11/16		Day was spent erecting tents in Moascar Camp. General troops were under orders of Division and Corps	
"	2/11/16			
"	3/11/16		Ditto	
"	4/11/16		Ditto	
"	5/11/16		Ditto	
"	6/11/16		Ditto	
"	7/11/16		Ditto	
"	8/11/16		Ditto	
"	9/11/16		Ditto	
"	10/11/16		Ditto	
"	11/11/16		Ditto	
"	12/11/16		Ditto	
"	13/11/16		Ditto	
"	14/11/16		Ditto	
"	15/11/16		Ditto	
"	16/11/16		Ditto	

R.H. Campbell Pitson O.C. X/18TMB

Army Form C. 2118.

WAR DIARY
or
INTELLIGENCE SUMMARY.
(Erase heading not required.)

Instructions regarding War Diaries and Intelligence Summaries are contained in F.S. Regs., Part II. and the Staff Manual respectively. Title pages will be prepared in manuscript.

Place	Date	Hour	Summary of Events and Information	Remarks and references to Appendices
Mannel Camp	17/11/16		All personnel of Battery employed on Div. + Corps fatigues	
	18/11/16		DITTO	
	19/11/16		DITTO	
	20/11/16		DITTO	
	21/11/16		DITTO	
	22/11/16		DITTO	
	23/11/16		All men employed on fatigues were returned to the Battery to day.	
	24/11/16		Parade and inspection of whole Battery	
	25/11/16		Employed: Breaking dug out in Camp. + Parade in WH order	
	26/11/16		Five men sent to Brigade form W/L HTMB.	
	27/11/16		Guns + hand carts overhauled + inspected	
	28/11/16		Drill Parade order, started at 9.45PM. To march to DAOURS	
	29/11/16		Drill Parade today arrived DAOURS at 6.45AM Bivouacked day	
	30/11/16		Started at 8.00AM for LA CHAUSSÉ, arriving at 3.15PM Billeted	

R.R. Campbell Jasson
O.C. ✗ / 6 T.M.B.

8th, Division.

X/8, T. M. Battery.

December, 1916.

Army Form C. 2118.

WAR DIARY
or
INTELLIGENCE SUMMARY.

(Erase heading not required.)

Instructions regarding War Diaries and Intelligence Summaries are contained in F.S. Regs., Part II. and the Staff Manual respectively. Title pages will be prepared in manuscript.

Place	Date	Hour	Summary of Events and Information	Remarks and references to Appendices
			Confidential War Diary of X/3 Trench Mortar Battery From 1-12-16 To 31-12-16 Vol (3)	

Army Form C. 2118.

WAR DIARY
or
INTELLIGENCE SUMMARY.
(Erase heading not required.)

Instructions regarding War Diaries and Intelligence Summaries are contained in F. S. Regs., Part II. and the Staff Manual respectively. Title pages will be prepared in manuscript.

Place	Date	Hour	Summary of Events and Information	Remarks and references to Appendices
LINE OF MARCH	1-12-16		Line of March	
"	2-12-16		DITTO	
ANDAINVILLE	3-12-16		Rest. Billeted in Andainville	
"	4-12-16		DITTO	
"	5-12-16		DITTO	
"	6-12-16		DITTO	
"	7-12-16		DITTO	
"	8-12-16		DITTO	
"	9-12-16		DITTO	
Line of March	10-12-16		Marched from Andainville to Fienvillers Battery billeted	
FIENVILLERS	11-12-16		Battery started training. Drill, Revolver exercise etc	
"	12-12-16		Training, Route marches, football-matches etc	
"	13-12-16		DITTO	
"	14-12-16		DITTO	
"	15-12-16		DITTO	
"	16-12-16		DITTO	
"	17-12-16		DITTO	

Army Form C. 2118.

WAR DIARY
or
INTELLIGENCE SUMMARY.
(Erase heading not required.)

Place	Date	Hour	Summary of Events and Information	Remarks and references to Appendices
RIOMER	18-12-16		TRAINING. DRILL. ROUTE-MARCHES	
	19-12-16		Ditto	
	20-12-16		Ditto	
	21-12-16		Ditto	
	22-12-16		Ditto	
	23-12-16		Ditto	
	24-12-16		Ditto	
	25-12-16		Battery football match	
	26-12-16		TRAINING	
	27-12-16		Ditto	
	28-12-16		Ditto	
	29-12-16		Ditto Line of march RIOMER — St SAUVEUR	
	30-12-16		Line of march St SAUVEUR — VAUX	
	31-12-16		Line of march VAUX — Camp 14	

R.L.Campbell Major 2 Lieut
OC X/1STMB

8th, Division.

23rd, T. M. Battery.

17/8/16 to 31/8/16.

23rd T. M. Battery.

War Diary

17-8-16 — 31-8-16.

Vol I

Army Form C. 2118.

WAR DIARY
or
INTELLIGENCE SUMMARY.
(Erase heading not required.)

Instructions regarding War Diaries and Intelligence Summaries are contained in F. S. Regs., Part II. and the Staff Manual respectively. Title pages will be prepared in manuscript.

Place	Date	Hour	Summary of Events and Information	Remarks and references to Appendices
In the field	17-8-16	—	Mortars in line :- 8. Casualties :- Nil. Ammunition expended :- 403 rounds. Right Sector :- Our mortars were very active, and shelled enemy trenches constantly, retaliation was weak. Work was continued on two new emplacements. Left Sector :- Enemy trenches were heavily shelled; also two a.p. heads, while a wiring party was dispersed. Headcover was put on new emplacement.	
"	18-8-16	—	Mortars in line :- 8. Casualties :- Nil. Amm. exp. :- 409 rounds. Right Sector :- Enemy were more active, specially with the minenwerfer. We retaliated vigorously throughout the night. One of our emplacements under construction was destroyed by enemy shell fire. Material for head cover was carried up throughout the night. Left Sector :- Our mortars in this sector have been very busy. We silenced a machine gun opp. G.4.4. and a wiring party in front of "Little Willie", and shelled enemy s.p. heads at intervals throughout the night.	
"	19-8-16	—	Mortars in line :- 8. Casualties :- Nil. Amm. exp. :- 299 rounds. Right Sector :- Very quiet during last 24 hours. We disposed a working party at 2.30 a.m. and completed new emplacement at G.4.d.7¾.1.	

Place	Date	Hour	Summary of Events and Information	Remarks and references to Appendices
In the field	19-8-16 Cont.	—	Left Sector: As batt'n in this front were working in trenches, we fired only in retaliation, shelling his trenches heavily whenever he opened fire. Steel covers were put up on new position at G.4.d.2.8½.	
"			Mortars in line :- 8. Casualties :- Nil. Amm. exp. 397 rounds.	
"			Right Sector :- Enemy were more active in this sector with R.G.s., T.M.s and aerial darts. We bombarded his trenches at 11:30 p.m. between 3 a.m. and 4 a.m. and again about 5 a.m. At 2:25 a.m. we fired 10 rounds on hostile working party at S.5.c.2.4.	
"	20-8-16	—	Left Sector :- About 8:45 p.m. enemy started a vigorous bombardment of our trenches with T.M.s., R.G.s and minenwerfers. We replied with all guns, and enemy remained quiet during remainder of night.	
"			Mortars in line :- 8. Casualties :- Nil. Amm. exp. - 339 rounds.	
"			Right Sector :- Completed new emplacement at G.4.C. 7¾.¾. and registered from it.	
"	21-8-16	—	Left Sector :- From 6 p.m. to 7:15 p.m. enemy searched all our positions with 4.2 shells, but without success. About midnight, we caught one of his working parties in little Willie.	

WAR DIARY or INTELLIGENCE SUMMARY

Army Form C. 2118.

Place	Date	Hour	Summary of Events and Information	Remarks and references to Appendices
In the field	22-8-16	—	Mortars in line :- 8 Casualties - Nil Ammo exp - 420 rounds. Right Sector :- Everything normal and retaliation for our firing only slight. Our mortars silenced a M.G. at G.5.c.5.2½, and afterwards dispersed a working party about G.5.c.2.3. Left Sector :- In this sector, we registered one of our guns on roofing part on lip of a crater, and fired on it at intervals. We also shelled enemy trenches intermittently throughout the night.	
"	23-8-16	—	Battery was relieved today, and marched back to rest billets 2/Lieut A.S. Fockett 2/M Leakr left the battery this morning to join M.G. Corps at Grantham. Two mortars were left with 25/T.M. Battery as per instructions	
"	24-8-16	—	Two mortars were sent to 8th Div. School of Mortars today. All guns were cleaned and inspected and deficiencies noted. Four guns were with personnel for same under Capt ?? B D... left at 2 p.m for trenches to work in conjunction with 26/T.M Battery	
"	25-8-16	—	Party returned from trenches without casualties. Men were instructed in rifle drill and gun drill, and all new kit and equipment was issued to battery	

Army Form C. 2118.

WAR DIARY
or
INTELLIGENCE SUMMARY.

(Erase heading not required.)

Instructions regarding War Diaries and Intelligence Summaries are contained in F. S. Regs., Part II. and the Staff Manual respectively. Title pages will be prepared in manuscript.

4

Place	Date	Hour	Summary of Events and Information	Remarks and references to Appendices
In the field	26-8-16	—	Kit, equipment and clothing inspection was held today. Kits tidy and fairly complete. All steel helmets were collected and sent to be sanded and painted. No 13892 Pte H. Clarke 2/Sco. Rif. was tried by Commanding Officer 2/Sco. Rif. and was recommended for a G.C.M. In this connection Lt W. Baxton 23/T.M. Battery was detailed as prosecutor.	
"	27-8-16	—	Nothing of interest to report.	
"	28-8-16	—	Nothing of interest to report. Men have been allowed to rest during the last two days.	
"	29-8-16	—	This morning the following officer, N.C.O. and men joined the Battery. 2/Lieut Edmund Cecil Jacks 2/Devon Regt. No 5343 Sgt G Shack 2/W. Yorks R. No 16393 Pte J Warren 3/W. Yorks R. No 9089 Pte H Silk 2/Middx R. No 10751 Pte R Rhys 2/Sco. Rif. All steel helmets were returned today having been sanded and painted.	
"	30-8-16	—	Usual parades. Battery was had out and sections 1 + 3 warned to parade for trenches the following morning at 8 a.m. Battery talked at 5 p.m.	
"	31-8-16	—	Sections 1 + 3 relieved the 25/T.M. Battery in trenches today. All mortars last to 8th Divisional School of Mortars were returned today, as School is being	

Army Form C. 2118.

WAR DIARY
or
INTELLIGENCE SUMMARY
(Erase heading not required.)

Place	Date	Hour	Summary of Events and Information	Remarks and references to Appendices
In the field	31-8-16	—	wound up the following N.C.O. and man returned from School of Battery today. Sgt Sear 9/Middx R. Pte Ridley 7/W. Yorks R. Thomas B. Duncan Capt. %c 23/T.M. Battery	

8th, Division.

24th, T. M. Battery.

August, 1916.

Army Form C. 2118.

24th Trench Mortar Battery

WAR DIARY
or
INTELLIGENCE SUMMARY.
(Erase heading not required.)

Instructions regarding War Diaries and Intelligence Summaries are contained in F.S. Regs., Part II. and the Staff Manual respectively. Title pages will be prepared in manuscript.

Place	Date	Hour	Summary of Events and Information	Remarks and references to Appendices
	AUG 1916			
Fosse 9. ANNEQUIN	1.		½ Batt'y in trenches (GUINCHY sector) (½ in Fosse 9. Nothing to report beyond the usual T.M. activity in retaliation for enemy's rifle grenades, dabs rc.	
	2.		Nothing to report.	
	3.		The enemy shelled Fosse 9. Causing 3 casualties. One killed & two slightly wounded. ½ Batt's in trenches was relieved. Nothing to report in his.	
	4.		Day Quiet. In evening we dropped a T.M. in enemy bombing post causing much damage & several casualties. The enemy retaliated heavily with T.Ms. darts, rifle grenades rc. A T.M. duel continued intermittently all night. The battery was relieved by the 23rd T.M.B. at 11.0.C. & proceeded to billets at BEUVRY.	
	5.		Fosse 9. was again shelled, but no damage was done.	
BEUVRY	6.		Nothing to report beyond the usual battery parades.	
	7.		In the morning No 2 sect'n relieved 25th T.M.B in the HULLUCH sector trenches The relief was very unsatisfactory & the ranges & lay of the guns handed over were unreliable resulting in a mortar falling in one of our own saps & causing one casualty. One officer of the 25th T.M.B remained in trenches to give information. The attitude of the enemy was Quiet unless	

Army Form C. 2118.

WAR DIARY
or
INTELLIGENCE SUMMARY.
(Erase heading not required.)

24th J/76 G.B.

Place	Date	Hour	Summary of Events and Information	Remarks and references to Appendices
	AUG. 1916.			
BUVRY.	7th Contd		disturbed when he retaliated heavily on our cops his ranges of which he had perfectly	
	8.		Nothing to report beyond usual T.M. duels.	
HULLUCH SECTOR TRENCHES	9.		— Do —	
	10.		In the afternoon carried out a bombardment of the enemy's line in conjunction with the Medium T.Ms. with satisfactory results.	
	11.		No. 2 section relieved No. 1. in trenches. Nothing to report.	
	12.		Nothing to report beyond usual T.M. duels. At 9 P.M. we exploded two mines but little action followed.	
	13.		Enemy were to-day much more active with T.Ms. causing several casualties in the front line. On the right the enemy carried out a raid but wounded. was bombed back.	
	14.		The battery was relieved by the 25th Bde T.M.B. Nothing to report.	
NOYELLES Billet FOUQUEREUIL.	15.		Battery proceeded to billets at FOUQUEREUIL.	
	16.		Nothing to report beyond usual battery parades.	

Army Form C. 2118.

WAR DIARY
or
INTELLIGENCE SUMMARY.
(Erase heading not required.)

24th J.M. G.B.

Instructions regarding War Diaries and Intelligence Summaries are contained in F. S. Regs., Part II. and the Staff Manual respectively. Title pages will be prepared in manuscript.

Place	Date	Hour	Summary of Events and Information	Remarks and references to Appendices
	AUG. 1916			
BILLETS AT	17.		Nothing to report beyond usual battery parades.	
FOUQUEREUIL	18.		Do.	
	19.		Do.	
	20.		Do.	
	21.		Do.	
	22.		No 2 section moved up to billets in VERMELLES prior to taking over trenches. No 1 section moved next day (23rd).	
VERMELLES	23.		No 2 section relieved the 43rd Bpd. T.Ms. in the HOHENZOLLERN REDOUBT. The enemy bombarded our trenches during the night with artillery owing to an attack that was taking place on the left.	
HOHENZOLLERN TRENCHES	24.		The enemy were active during the afternoon with T.Ms. & artillery mostly on our communication trenches: We retaliated heavily with Stokes & medium T.Ms. & eventually silenced him. During the night, after a very heavy bombardment of the enemy's trenches, which we carried out prior to a raid, he retaliated with artillery & T.Ms. of all calibres on our second line damaging our trenches considerably in several places.	

Army Form C. 2118.

WAR DIARY
or
INTELLIGENCE SUMMARY.
(Erase heading not required.)

24th J. 96. B.

Instructions regarding War Diaries and Intelligence Summaries are contained in F.S. Regs., Part II. and the Staff Manual respectively. Title pages will be prepared in manuscript.

Place	Date	Hour	Summary of Events and Information	Remarks and references to Appendices
HOHENZOLLERN TRENCHES.	AUG. 1916.			
	25		Nothing to report beyond the usual T.M. activity during the day. The night was extremely quiet on account of wiring parties being out.	
	26.		Nothing to report. No 2 section was relieved by No.1 section.	
	27.		Nothing to report beyond usual T.M. activity.	
	28.		At 12.30 we carried out a pre-arranged bombardment of the enemy's front line & trench junctions in co-operation with the medium T.Ms. & supported by the six inch Howitzer battery. The operation was successful & the enemy's retaliation very small.	
	29.		At 3 P.M. we carried out a heavy bombardment of the enemy's trenches in co-operation with the medium T.Ms. & the artillery. The operation was successful although hindered by an extremely heavy thunderstorm & rain & high wind. The enemy hardly retaliated at all.	
	30.		No. 2 section relieved No.1 section. All trenches in extremely bad condition on account of heavy rains. At 6 Ac.P.M. carried out a bombardment of the enemy's front line trenches in co-operation with the medium T.Ms. Observation of result was impossible owing to mist & rain, but there was very little retaliation	

Army Form C. 2118.

WAR DIARY
or
INTELLIGENCE SUMMARY.
(Erase heading not required.)

24th of J.M.B.

Instructions regarding War Diaries and Intelligence Summaries are contained in F. S. Regs., Part II. and the Staff Manual respectively. Title pages will be prepared in manuscript.

Place	Date	Hour	Summary of Events and Information	Remarks and references to Appendices
HOHENZOLLERN TRENCHES.	AUG. 1916. 30. cont'd.		A faulty shell had to be abandoned in No 2 gun emplacement, whilst it blew up, damaging the gun beyond repair. The enemy obtained a direct hit on No.1. gun emplacement with a heavy T.M. & blew it in without damaging the gun. The night was comparatively quiet, beyond the continual occasional shots as directed on that part of the enemy's front line we had bombarded during the day in the hope of catching working party. At 4.15 A.M. the enemy exploded a mine & a flying sandbag entered No 3 gun emplacement, & alighting on the elevating stand of the gun, so damaged it as to render the gun useless. We sustained no casualties.	
	31.		Nothing to report beyond the usual occasional shots fired to harass the enemy throughout the day. Night quiet on account of working parties.	

8th, Division.

25th, T. M. Battery.

August, 1916.

Army Form C. 2118

WAR DIARY
or
INTELLIGENCE SUMMARY
(Erase heading not required.)

Vol 1

War Diary
of
The 25 Light Trench Mortar Battery

WAR DIARY
or
INTELLIGENCE SUMMARY
(Erase heading not required.)

Army Form C. 2118

Place	Date	Hour	Summary of Events and Information	Remarks and references to Appendices
VERMELLES	1/8/16	5pm	A successful bombardment was carried out against the enemy when he had cut our wire of our Brigade near craters, also on extreme right of our Brigade near BOYEAU 94.	
	2/8/16	3pm	During afternoon mortars were brought into position & at 4.30pm we opened a heavy fire on enemy trenches between G.5.C.7½ & G.5.D.1.2.	
	3/8/16	5pm	We bombed G.5.D.1.2. when this was a M.G. emplacement and had as target was not visible cannot say with what result.	
	4/8/16		The right of Brigade front during last 24 hours 075 n 100 rounds were fired in retaliation & over 100 in defensives.	

Army Form C. 2118

WAR DIARY
or
INTELLIGENCE SUMMARY
(Erase heading not required.)

Instructions regarding War Diaries and Intelligence Summaries are contained in F. S. Regs., Part II. and the Staff Manual respectively. Title Pages will be prepared in manuscript.

Place	Date	Hour	Summary of Events and Information	Remarks and references to Appendices
HOHEN-ZOLLERN SECTION	5/8/16		During day, 338 rounds were expended on "Special Points".	
	6/8/16		A quiet day. We fired over 500 rounds, with like retaliation.	
FOUQUER-UEIL	7/8/16		Battery went into bivouac at FOUQUEREUIL breaking the journey at SAILLY-LA-BOURSE.	
	8/8/16		Day spent in cleaning & fatigues.	
	9/8/16		Programme of work was sent in.	
	10/8/16		Programme carried out. Cricket match in afternoon.	
	11/8/16		(Men spent morning at Baths).	
	12/8/16		Day spent on Rifle Range.	
	13/8/16		Lectures & Instruction in use of Gas Helmets.	

Army Form C. 2118

WAR DIARY
or
INTELLIGENCE SUMMARY
(Erase heading not required.)

Place	Date	Hour	Summary of Events and Information	Remarks and references to Appendices
FOUQUER- VEIL	14/8/16		Captain A.C. TAYLOR & Lt. S.J. HAWKES visit trenches with a view of taking over on following day.	
	15/8/16		Four guns & personnel moved up into the trenches.	
	16/8/16		H.Qrs. & Battery & remaining personnel moved into Bghn Redoubt.	
QUARRIES SECTION	17/8/16		The Battery fires 002 in MOYELLES. A good day's shooting was done.	
	18/8/16		Considerable damage done to enemy lines & our guns firing from BORDER REDOUBT.	
	19/8/16		A good day in the line. Over 600 rounds were fired.	

Army Form C. 2118

WAR DIARY
or
INTELLIGENCE SUMMARY
(Erase heading not required.)

Instructions regarding War Diaries and Intelligence Summaries are contained in F. S. Regs., Part II. and the Staff Manual respectively. Title Pages will be prepared in manuscript.

Place	Date	Hour	Summary of Events and Information	Remarks and references to Appendices
QUARRIES SECTION	20/8/16	5pm	We bombarded the enemy's saps behind the HAIRPIN	
	21/8/16		547 rounds were fired in this day with good results.	
	22/8/16	1pm	In conjunction with the MEDIUM 7.7's we bombarded the Huns trench G.5.c.9.4.	
	23/8/16		Our guns were very active bombarding saps during the night.	
	24/8/16		All guns were massed in BOYEAU 80 & registered on the enemy's trench which we are raiding tonight.	
	24-25/8/16	12 mn	We bombarded the enemy's trenches raided by us firing over 1200 rounds. We sustained 3 casualties.	

1875 Wt. W593/826 1,000,000 4/15 J.B.C. & A. A.D.S.S./Forms/C. 2118.

WAR DIARY
or
INTELLIGENCE SUMMARY
(Erase heading not required.)

Army Form C. 2118

Place	Date	Hour	Summary of Events and Information	Remarks and references to Appendices
QUARRIES SECTION	26/8/16		We retaliated energetically to enemy bombardment.	
	27/8/16		We carried out various shoots on enemy "TENDER SPOTS"	
	28/8/16	3 pm	Fired in conjunction with Medium T.M's opposite G.12.5.	
	29/8/16		Very bad weather was experienced preventing us from doing much firing.	
	30/8/16		Four of our men were killed by shell explosion whilst an Emplacement was being worked.	
	31/8/16		Our gun which was buried by explosion was dug out. Base Plate still missing.	

Archibald Douglas Cuffe
OC 25th Trench Mortar Batty.

8th, Division.

8th, T. M. Battery.

June , 1916.

Army Form C. 2118.

8th T.M. Battery

WAR DIARY
or
INTELLIGENCE SUMMARY.
(Erase heading not required.)

Vol 2

Instructions regarding War Diaries and Intelligence Summaries are contained in F.S. Regs., Part II. and the Staff Manual respectively. Title pages will be prepared in manuscript.

Place	Date	Hour	Summary of Events and Information	Remarks and references to Appendices
Chada-Boom at Berthen	June 1/16 – 11/6/16		Battery in training	Cld
Reninghelst Trench No 28	June 11	7.45pm	Moved to RENINGHELST.	Cld
	12/6/16	12 m.n.	Relieved 9th T.M.B. Night quiet.	Cld
do	13/6/16	2 a.m.	Our artillery fired heavily on German positions on our left. The enemy did not retaliate on our sector.	Cld
		1 pm	Enemy fired a few trench mortar shells into T.19. Our mortars retaliated. Rest of day quiet.	Cld
do	14/6/16	12 noon	Only a few trench mortar shells were fired into our sector. We retaliated on PICCADILLY FARM	Cld
do	15/6/16	3 pm	The enemy were most very active with Trench Mortars from Lt E101 crater. We retaliated on the right & left of crater but were unable to reach main one.	Cld
do	16/6/16	2 pm	Enemy trench mortars active over all our front. We retaliated. Heavy artillery fire on both sides from 11pm – 1 a.m.	Cld
do	17/6/16	1.45pm	Aeroplane activity. Enemy mortars active. Night quiet.	Cld

Army Form C. 2118.

8th T.M. Battery

WAR DIARY
or
INTELLIGENCE SUMMARY
(Erase heading not required.)

Instructions regarding War Diaries and Intelligence Summaries are contained in F. S. Regs., Part II. and the Staff Manual respectively. Title pages will be prepared in manuscript.

Place	Date	Hour	Summary of Events and Information	Remarks and references to Appendices
Trenches G-28	18/6/16	3 pm	Morning quiet. A little artillery fire on both sides. CWS	
		5 pm	Effectually silenced mortars in No 2 Crater. Two guns firing on No 3 Crater in co-operation with light artillery. Enemy seen to leave main crater & retire. Rounds expended 160. CWS	
do	19/6/16	1 pm	A few M.B. exchanged by mortars. CWS	
		5 pm	Fired heavily on No 3 Crater until enemy mortars were silenced. Rounds expended 150. CWS	
do	20/6/16	3 pm	Mortars fairly active. Rounds expended 50. CWS	
do	21/6/16	2 am	Relieved by 6th T.M.B. (Canadian) arrived ST. MARTIN'S au LAERT at 4 pm. CWS	
St Martin's au Laert	22/6/16 – 30/6/16		Battery in training. CWS	
	30.6.16			C.W. Sawyer 2Lt OC. 8th T.M.B.

8th, Division.

Y/8, Medium T. M. Battery.

September, 1916.

WAR DIARY
or
~~INTELLIGENCE SUMMARY.~~
(Erase heading not required.)

Army Form C. 2118.

CONFIDENTIAL

War Diary
of
Y/8 Medium Trench Mortar Battery
from 1.9.16 to 30.9.16

Volume I

N.B. War diary for this month to be sent by 1.12.16

Army Form C. 2118.

WAR DIARY
or
INTELLIGENCE SUMMARY. of 1/1/8 T.M.B.

(Erase heading not required.)

Place	Date	Hour	Summary of Events and Information	Remarks and references to Appendices
2 Bays in action at Wn trench one to O.B.1 New Bast Acting 1/4 to L.R. Bryan H.Shunzellan Station	1.9.16	3-3.30 pm	Casualties nil Ammunition expended 45 rds. Tactical Report 14 rds. fired at O.B.1 during afternoon 3 - 3.30 pm 31 rds fired per Co. operation with Stokes on G.4 + H.3 H.2 + G.4 + H.2. 7½ LITTLE WILLIE Many direct hits on parapet. No enemy retaliation	Report made by Lt Parkman. OC 1/8 TMB

WAR DIARY
INTELLIGENCE SUMMARY. Y/8 T.M.B.

(Erase heading not required.)

Army Form C. 2118.

Place	Date	Hour	Summary of Events and Information	Remarks and references to Appendices
Millencourt Sector	2.9.16		of Y/8 T.M.B.	

Casualties nil.

Ammunition Newly expended,
60 rounds were fired at CROSS TRENCH and LITTLE WILLIE
* before enemy got away his trenches.
A fair amount of enemy artillery and trench
fire was drawn from about 7 to twelve noon to day.

CONFIDENTIAL PARTS. W.K. defence & Defensive flat ironmongery have come up to
the gun pit and fast are quickly disposed of pyro.
Ten containing S.A. cartridges in many cases only contain
three cartridges instead of six. (Two flash ink him hands)-
9 Phosphor or Dr Smoke.-   Reply to T. Paulin
9 now Hymns patently   Y/8 T.M.B.
                1 box cordensel fuel complete.
                1 Tail
                90 cartridges S.A.
                4 Guzji Newton.

Army Form C. 2118.

WAR DIARY
or
INTELLIGENCE SUMMARY. 1/8 M.B

(Erase heading not required.)

Place	Date	Hour	Summary of Events and Information	Remarks and references to Appendices
Hamilton Subs	3.9.16		Canadian and American Exploded 21+.	
Gun G in Cannock Rd.			**Tactical Report** Gun G fired 3 rounds in dark batting LITTLE WILLIE No more rounds been fired owing to fog.	
Gun F in Left Bogus			Fired 31 rds. Mines and Explosives in HOGS BACK CRATER. Heavy bombardment was Influenced. Very heavy attacks in bright upon us by our front about	
		11.30 am	" They mounted have firing.	
		2.30 pm	PO	
			By Lt Ricketts OC 1/8 M.B	

Army Form C. 2118.

WAR DIARY
or
INTELLIGENCE SUMMARY   4/18 MB

(Erase heading not required.)

Place	Date	Hour	Summary of Events and Information	Remarks and references to Appendices
Hebuterne Sector	4/9/16		Reconnoitre and Ammunition expends a 30.	
E Sec. 64 Bank Alley (in O.B.1)			TACTICAL REPORT 10 Mds. fire from at CROSS TRENCH during 24 hours for officers and disposing of enemy found.	
F Sec in Left Bryan Gun Through Alley		3-4 pm	Out of action, rifle withdrawn etc. 20 rds. rapid fire from at LITTLE WILLIE between 3 and 4 pm for destruction of enemy post house + use.	
			Duplicate of Report for 5.9.16 seems lost. CE	By Lt. Pickman O.C. 4/18 MB

Army Form C. 2118.

WAR DIARY
or
INTELLIGENCE SUMMARY.
(Erase heading not required.)

Place	Date	Hour	Summary of Events and Information	Remarks and references to Appendices
HOHENZOLLERN SECTOR	5.9.16		Army Report. Rounds fired 51 Casualties nil. Tactical. LITTLE WILLIE was ?unloaded. Three tins of oil were thrown into the air.	

Army Form C. 2118.

WAR DIARY
or
INTELLIGENCE SUMMARY   Y/S Trub

(Erase heading not required.)

Instructions regarding War Diaries and Intelligence
Summaries are contained in F. S. Regs., Part II.
and the Staff Manual respectively. Title Pages
will be prepared in manuscript.

Place	Date	Hour	Summary of Events and Information	Remarks and references to Appendices
Hohenzollern Sector	10/4/16		Eighteen pounds fired since now yesterday. Ammunition got	
E. Secⁿ in D.A.			No gun fired. 8 Adv.—on the Ypres. At this period little firing was done in all. The area was not looking dead in Aug.—Oct.	
				Officer Com 1st RFA Y/S Trub.

2449 Wt. W14957/Mgo 750,000 1/16 J.B.C. & A. Forms/C.2118/12.

WAR DIARY

or

INTELLIGENCE SUMMARY Y/8 TMB

Army Form C. 2118.

Place	Date	Hour	Summary of Events and Information	Remarks and references to Appendices
HOHENZ-LRN SECTOR	7.9.16		Number of rounds fired are yesterday upon 35. Chief Target - HOGS BACK (CRATER). At Mr. Line the shots possible to push the actual craters as we were not able to know left enough. Observation nil.	

C. M. Y/8 TMB

Army Form C. 2118.

WAR DIARY
or
INTELLIGENCE SUMMARY Y/E TMB

(Erase heading not required.)

Place	Date	Hour	Summary of Events and Information	Remarks and references to Appendices
	6.9.16		Rounds fired 2224 how yesterday +4. Shutters during the firing last night. Our guns fired during the morning & night. Quiet. The Boch calm. CASUALTIES Nil. Some shots fired reported from E spur (Infantry code) due to & (Infantry code). C.S. 217 AFA Y/EAB	

WAR DIARY or INTELLIGENCE SUMMARY Y/8 T.M.B

Army Form C. 2118.

Place	Date	Hour	Summary of Events and Information	Remarks and references to Appendices
HOHEN ZOLLERN SECTOR	9.4.16		Casualty Report – Nil	
			Ammunition Expended from noon yesterday till noon today	
F in O.B.1 apparatus		12 noon	TACTICAL REPORT	
F in left Bogan			E.F. & G guns fired in Co-operation with the Stokes Mortars.	
Ra M Crampley		2.20 am	E.F. & G guns fired 30 and 28 rounds respectively for Barrage fire on enemy front and right and left of enemy party for retaliation and registration.	
			19 rounds fired in this affair.	
			Lt. Parkman was shot dead almost instantaneously. On this afternoon fire and Cpl. Blunderbury was shot low and was slightly wounded, the bullet grazing his neck.	
			By H. Parkman OC. Y/8 T.M.B.

Army Form C. 2118.

WAR DIARY
or
INTELLIGENCE SUMMARY

(Erase heading not required.)

Place	Date	Hour	Summary of Events and Information	Remarks and references to Appendices
HOUPLINES SECTOR	10.9.16		Rounds fired since last Holiday 224, 23. Lt Packman was buried in the new portion of Vieille Militaire Cemetery and a wooden Cross erected over his grave.	C/Mn 4th M. H.R.T.B.

Instructions regarding War Diaries and Intelligence Summaries are contained in F. S. Regs., Part II. and the Staff Manual respectively. Title Pages will be prepared in manuscript.

WAR DIARY
or
~~INTELLIGENCE~~ SUMMARY
(Erase heading not required.)

Army Form C. 2118.

Y/8 T.M.B.

Place	Date	Hour	Summary of Events and Information	Remarks and references to Appendices
HOHENZOLLERN SECTOR	11-9-16		60 rounds fired in co-operation with the STOKES since yesterday. Our fire was mainly offensive. The chief targets were LITTLE WILLIE and the enemy's second line. CASUALTIES NIL C. [illegible] 2nd Lt RFA Y/8 T.M.B.	

2449 Wt. W14957/M90 750,000 1/16 J.B.C. & A. Forms/C.2118/12.

WAR DIARY

INTELLIGENCE SUMMARY 1/8 T.M.B.

Army Form C. 2118.

Place	Date	Hour	Summary of Events and Information	Remarks and references to Appendices
Hohenzollern Redoubt	29.1.16		60 Mtr fired once into Yesterday. About 10 perts came to mend — German Support line. This day shot arose one gun was buried with its detachment of Bolt 2 men — Gn Hall and Hawthorn were taken out alive, a pte of the help of men were taken to F.A. Station. Some prisoners and were taken	Sdr. J. Hall OC 1/8 TMB

WAR DIARY or INTELLIGENCE SUMMARY

Army Form G. 2118.

Place	Date	Hour	Summary of Events and Information	Remarks and references to Appendices
Wancourt Sector	19.4.16		Rounds fired from Yelverton now 14. Chief Target HINDENBURG & FOSSE TRENCHES. It is only possible to fire by map at the second line on the sector on account of German front line trenches being on reverse of the summit. CASUALTIES Nil.	

Lieut. RFC OC
Wancourt 9/18 Bty

Army Form C. 2118.

WAR DIARY
or
INTELLIGENCE SUMMARY H/E They
(Erase heading not required.)

Place	Date	Hour	Summary of Events and Information	Remarks and references to Appendices
	14.9.16		Bn. found L.Y. Chief I.- Heavy messages on a left.	

WAR DIARY or INTELLIGENCE SUMMARY

Y/1 T.M.B.

Place	Date	Hour	Summary of Events and Information	Remarks and references to Appendices
Hénencourt Redoubt H-10			Rounds fired Once. Yesterday noon #4. Shot target - Heavy newsweeper opposite left of our front. One other was reported observed.	

2/Lieut R.F.K.
O.C. Y/1 T.M.B.

Army Form C. 2118.

WAR DIARY
or
INTELLIGENCE SUMMARY   Y/8 TMB

(Erase heading not required.)

Place	Date	Hour	Summary of Events and Information	Remarks and references to Appendices
Hebuterne Sect.	15.9.16		Roads found and a yesterday were. The roofs were full expenditure of ammunition was due to a dozen of Shri at a much as possible at that particular time. The detachments were also fruitful employed making dugouts and head-cover. C. Mc. 7/Lt - 2 Lt OC Y/8 TMB	Y/8 TMB

WAR DIARY or INTELLIGENCE SUMMARY

Army Form C. 2118.

Place	Date	Hour	Summary of Events and Information	Remarks and references to Appendices
Thuzillers Sector	16.9.16		Casualties nil. Rounds fired since yesterday 38. A steady rate of fire was kept up during three days. Also many attacks were daily arranged in conjunction with Stokes. One noticed that the strokes mortar generally fired a good while before ours. Perhaps a time limit might be arranged for both. A.S.R. 2/Lt R.F.A. OC Y/51 M.B.	

WAR DIARY

INTELLIGENCE SUMMARY 1/8 7th B

Army Form C. 2118.

Place	Date	Hour	Summary of Events and Information	Remarks and references to Appendices
Armentieres Sector	14.9.16		Rounds fired 53. Rounds p/s Shorts. A large number of rounds were fired at gun. On this day Rounds accumulated at gun were 334; on 15th there were 407.	

J.S.

Army Form C. 2118.

WAR DIARY
or
INTELLIGENCE SUMMARY

(Erase heading not required.)

21 S.T.M.B.

Place	Date	Hour	Summary of Events and Information	Remarks and references to Appendices
Ifezyll Sector	1/9/16		Rounds fired 50. A steady rate of fire. Casualties nil. S.C.	

WAR DIARY
INTELLIGENCE SUMMARY

Army Form C. 2118.

(Erase heading not required.)

7/6 7NB

Place	Date	Hour	Summary of Events and Information	Remarks and references to Appendices
Mouquet Farm	19.9.16		Rounds fired 51. Casualties nil. Tactical patrol sent out by 2/Lt. Stewart — Reconnoitred CROSS TRENCH and communication trench leading thereto with 20 men. with successful results judging by [amount?] of material thrown up. Also shelled LITTLE WILLIE and HINDENBURG TRENCH and afterwards with gun mounts — to the extent of thirty rounds.	e.g. OCY/STMS

2449 Wt. W14957/M90 750,000 1/16 J.B.C. & A. Forms/C.2118/12.

Army Form C. 2118.

WAR DIARY
or
INTELLIGENCE SUMMARY 4/8 NzB
(Erase heading not required.)

Place	Date	Hour	Summary of Events and Information	Remarks and references to Appendices
Holnon Sector	20.9.16		Casualties nil. Rounds fired 28. Tactical proposals report by 2nd Lieut Salusbury - "Jas Gladys LITTLE WILLIE + HINDENBURG TRENCHES + approaches but 28 rds. Caused considerable damage. Enemy Metallum seen for the did not so in the afternoon at all. C.E.	

WAR DIARY or INTELLIGENCE SUMMARY

Army Form C. 2118.

7/8 7hB

Place	Date	Hour	Summary of Events and Information	Remarks and references to Appendices
Hohenzollern Sector	21.9.16		No. 1 Coy fired A.G. Casualties nil. Tactical report by O/C Search :- "Fired LITTLE WILLIE from G.4.b.4.4 to S.4.b.3½.6½ enemy front line up gradually by traverse at flare up. Gun batter was flare up which closed comm. trench at G.4.b.43.68 and G.4.b.50.25 making it hard to see down the comm. trench for about 50 yds." C.S.	

WAR DIARY or INTELLIGENCE SUMMARY

Army Form C. 2118.

2/8 TWB

Place	Date	Hour	Summary of Events and Information	Remarks and references to Appendices
Maydan Sultan	22.9.16		Recs. nil.	
			Recs. fired 40.	
			Tactical reports by 2/L Scholes :—	
		5.30 p.m.	"5.30 p.m. we fired 32 rds. Bet. 94 2 4 2 4 & 94 f 3 f 69	
			LITTLE WILLIE. About 30 yds of trench & wire	
			was completely destroyed. Three dugouts were	
			blown up & & Turks hurt. The damage was	
			severe — the MGs have not being located, later	
			we fired 8 rounds with Smoke. shells & they were	
				lodged some (?) under	
				direct hits on trench."	
				C.I.

Army Form C. 2118.

WAR DIARY
or
INTELLIGENCE SUMMARY.
(Erase heading not required.)

Instructions regarding War Diaries and Intelligence Summaries are contained in F. S. Regs., Part II. and the Staff Manual respectively. Title pages will be prepared in manuscript.

Place	Date	Hour	Summary of Events and Information	Remarks and references to Appendices
HOHENZOLLERN REDOUBT	23.9.16		HINDENBERG TRENCH shelled with satisfactory results. Rounds fired 21. Bromette nil.	
	24.9.16		Continuous Trench Mortar duel during morning. Rounds fired 41. Bromette nil.	
	25.9.16		I. Knew activity of trench mortars from 7.30 AM to 11.30 AM. Rounds fired 102. Bromette nil.	
	26.9.16		Heavy trench mortar fighting since 9 am. Besieged enemys second line & fired continuously. Rounds fired 80. Bromette nil.	
	27.9.16		Retaliation to enemys "oil-cans" (fired from HOGS BACK). Rounds fired 68. Bromette nil.	
	28.9.16		"Oil-can" on HOGS BACK silenced directly it opened fire. Rounds fired 23. Bromette nil.	

WAR DIARY
INTELLIGENCE SUMMARY

Army Form C. 2118.

Place	Date	Hour	Summary of Events and Information	Remarks and references to Appendices
HOHENZOLLERN SECTOR			Reqt. M.G. & Trench Mortars relieved C.E.	
"	29.10.16		Am. Report. Rds. fired 61. Leinwetter ad Tactical report. Hog's Back Craters was shelled by enemy retaliation fire. We also shelled communication trench along much damage.	
"	30.10.16		Am. Report. Rds fired 59. Barralin nil Tactical Report. fired damage was done to HINDENBURG TRENCH. We also fired on communication trench from † LITTLE WILLIE to HINDENBURG TRENCH, † on HOG'S BACK CRATER.	

8th, Division.

Y/8, Medium T. M. Battery.

October, 1916.

CONFIDENTIAL

War Diary.

Y/8 Medium Trench Mortar Battery

From 1.10.16 to 31.10.16

Volume I

Army Form C. 2118.

WAR DIARY
or
INTELLIGENCE SUMMARY.
(Erase heading not required.)

Instructions regarding War Diaries and Intelligence Summaries are contained in F. S. Regs., Part II. and the Staff Manual respectively. Title pages will be prepared in manuscript.

Place	Date	Hour	Summary of Events and Information	Remarks and references to Appendices
HOHENZOLLERN SECTOR	1.10.16		Owen Report. Rounds fired by Casualties nil (1st) (2nd) HINDENBURGH TRENCH LITTLE WILLIE and A+B BACK CRATER shelled during the 24 hrs ending - noon 1.10.16 there were no firsts + support line trenches on fire first + support lines.	
"	2.10.16		Amm Report. Rounds fired 59. Casualties nil. Tactical Report. A+B BACK CRATER where enemy has been busy for past few days. Rain has on shelled. Also enemy front + supp lines (Hindenburg + Little willie) where enemy used to sweep same bridges. 30 rds were fired during night.	

T2134. Wt. W708-776. 500000. 4/15. Sir J. C. & S.

Army Form C. 2118.

WAR DIARY
or
INTELLIGENCE SUMMARY.
(Erase heading not required.)

Instructions regarding War Diaries and Intelligence Summaries are contained in F.S. Regs., Part II. and the Staff Manual respectively. Title pages will be prepared in manuscript.

Place	Date	Hour	Summary of Events and Information	Remarks and references to Appendices
HOHENZOLLERN REDOUBT	3.10.16		10 minutes fired on G.4.b.5.5. Junction offensive. Great damage to enemy's defences. Rapid fire on HOG'S BACK at times given by Division (for 3 minutes each). Enemy retaliated on QUARRY ALLEY. Enemy has been silenced. Rounds fired 63. Casualties nil.	
	4.10.16		Good shooting done at minenwerfer G.4.b.74.6.2. Rounds fired 25. Casualties nil.	
	5.10.16		Killed enemy's communication trench & front line at 2.44pm & 10.30pm. Enemy's retaliation feeble but his shooting was good. Rounds fired 26. Casualties 2nd Lt. Ellis wounded.	
	6.10.16		Cut trenches CROSS TRENCH, HINDENBURG & LITTLE WILLIE. Shelled HINDENBURG & approaches. Fired in accessory to Divisional programme. Rounds fired 252. Casualties nil.	
	7.10.16		Rapid fire at G.4.b.113.68 fired a rifle direct hits obtained. HOG'S BACK CRATER & LITTLE WILLIE shelled also minenwerfer at G.4.b. 35-97. Rounds fired 60. Casualties nil.	
	8.10.16		Considerable damage observed as result of firing on HOG'S BACK. Loopholes in LITTLE WILLIE fired on. Rounds fired 67. Casualties nil.	

Army Form C. 2118.

WAR DIARY
or
INTELLIGENCE SUMMARY.
(Erase heading not required.)

Instructions regarding War Diaries and Intelligence Summaries are contained in F. S. Regs., Part II. and the Staff Manual respectively. Title pages will be prepared in manuscript.

Place	Date	Hour	Summary of Events and Information	Remarks and references to Appendices
HOHENZOLLERN REDOUBT.	9/10/16		Loss Back crater fired on with much damage. Hindenburg Trench harassed & fished. Rounds fired 72. Casualties nil.	

Army Form C. 2118.

WAR DIARY
or
INTELLIGENCE SUMMARY.
(Erase heading not required.)

Instructions regarding War Diaries and Intelligence Summaries are contained in F. S. Regs., Part II. and the Staff Manual respectively. Title pages will be prepared in manuscript.

Place	Date	Hour	Summary of Events and Information	Remarks and references to Appendices
Hebuterne Rudolf 1st-3rd			[illegible heavy scribbles over text] with C.S.	
"	10.10.16		Army Report. Rounds fired 219. Casualties nil. Tactical Report. Enemy front & support lines weakly held & accompanied with very few snipers.	
	11.10.16		Army 16th carried out during day on HOGS BACK and HINDENBURG TRENCH but no enemy found. Fire 4.4.72.	
	12.10.16		ARMY REPORT 16 B/Rounds fired 51. CASUALTIES NIL. Enemy on HINDENBERG & HOGS BACK also on communicator trench retaliated with minenwerfer on LEFT BOYAU. Enemy retaliated with minenwerfer on LEFT BOYAU. No damage. Casualties nil.	

WAR DIARY
or
INTELLIGENCE SUMMARY.
(Erase heading not required.)

Army Form C. 2118.

Place	Date	Hour	Summary of Events and Information	Remarks and references to Appendices
HOHENZOLLERN REDOUBT.	13.10.16.		Wiring carried out on CROSS TRENCH and HINDENBERG. Several direct hits observed on material during night of 12th/13th on MUD ALLEY, but guns were not touched. Casualties nil. No. of rounds fired 64.	
	14.10.16.		Approaches to HINDENBERG trench from LITTLE WILLIE shelled. Firing carried out on HOG'S BACK CRATERS and HINDENBERG TRENCH. Enemy exceptionally quiet. Casualties nil. No. of rounds fired 60.	
	15.10.16		Bombardment of trenches from G.4.2.5.2 to G.4.2.5.3 according to Divisional programme. Hostile damage was observed as result of fire on HINDENBERG TRENCH. Enemy has several new mortars in line — light minenwerfer & light trench mortar. These have not been in action for some time. Casualties nil. No. of rounds fired 81.	
	16.10.16		Wiring carried out on HINDENBERG trench & LITTLE WILLIE. During firing on HOG'S BACK CRATER a number of bombs was thrown up. Enemy has been exceptionally quiet for the last 24 hours. Casualties nil. No. of rounds fired 46.	

Army Form C. 2118.

WAR DIARY
or
INTELLIGENCE SUMMARY.
(Erase heading not required.)

Instructions regarding War Diaries and Intelligence Summaries are contained in F. S. Regs., Part II. and the Staff Manual respectively. Title pages will be prepared in manuscript.

Place	Date	Hour	Summary of Events and Information	Remarks and references to Appendices
HOHENZOLLERN REDOUBT	17.10.16		Our position improved during morning.	
		4.30 pm	Enemy started heavy bombardment and "Rum-jar" fire on our lines. Rapid fire immediately carried out in conjunction with Stokes' gun. Enemy silenced. No. of rounds fired 67. Casualties nil.	
	18.10.16		Bombardment carried out in co-operation with Stokes' guns. Good shooting done. About forty rounds were fired in retaliation to enemy's fire. No. of rounds fired 84. Casualties nil.	
	19.10.16		Firing carried out in conjunction with Stokes guns. Direct hit on F gun position (LEFT BOYAU.) 50 rounds blown up. Mortars found could make a good gun position after a month or so. No. of rounds fired 38. Casualties nil.	
	20.10.16		Combined firing of Stokes' & howitzers on LITTLE WILLIE & HINDENBERG. Results satisfactory. No. of rounds fired 38. Casualties nil.	
	21.10.16		Firing carried out on HOG'S BACK & LITTLE WILLIE trench. Hits were observed. No. of rounds fired 30. Casualty :- 15761. Pte. BOWLER (R. BERKS) killed.	

Army Form C. 2118.

WAR DIARY
or
INTELLIGENCE SUMMARY.
(Erase heading not required.)

Instructions regarding War Diaries and Intelligence Summaries are contained in F. S. Regs., Part II. and the Staff Manual respectively. Title pages will be prepared in manuscript.

Place	Date	Hour	Summary of Events and Information	Remarks and references to Appendices
HOHENZOLLERN REDOUBT	22.10.16		Relieved by 21st DIVISION Anderson French Montana.	
	23.10.16		Battery moved to CITADEL camp (near FRICOURT)	
	23.10.16 to 31.10.16		Battery in rest at CITADEL Camp.	

8th, Division.

V/8, Heavy T. M. Battery.

September, 1916.

CONFIDENTIAL.

8th DIVISIONAL ARTILLERY.

WAR DIARY

OF

V/8 Heavy Trench Mortar Battery

From 1-9-16 To 30-9-16

(VOLUME 1.)

With APPENDICES Nos. None.

Army Form C. 2118.

WAR DIARY
INTELLIGENCE SUMMARY.

(Erase heading not required.)

1/8 Heavy Trench Mortar Battery

Diary commences 1st Sept 1916 as until beginning of August no War Diary had been kept. War Diary for August was made out by Divisional Trench Mortar Officer.

30.9.16.

WAR DIARY
INTELLIGENCE SUMMARY

(Erase heading not required.)

Army Form C. 2118.

Instructions regarding War Diaries and Intelligence Summaries are contained in F.S. Regs., Part II. and the Staff Manual respectively. Title pages will be prepared in manuscript.

Place	Date	Hour	Summary of Events and Information	Remarks and references to Appendices
Sally-le-Bosc	1.9.16		On this date the gun pit was still under the charge of the 1 Field Coy. Stone Counties R.E.	
	7.9.16		The pit was reported ready for use.	
	8.9.16		The gun fired. Thirteen rounds. Seven being directed against the South East corner of Sonons. There rounds were reported via. a field art. B.G. to have hit the target. The other six rounds were fired at enemy trench trenches positions. The results were good.	
	9.9.16		The pit was again under repair as the joints had been dislodges.	
	10.9.16		The gun was again fired at the afforsaid trench mortan. The workering of the gun was very difficult owing to the communications being all or insperable owing the 15 100 yds of wire being destroyed.	
	11.9.16		The pit was unable to helped until the 2.6 of the month, at which time the men were all employed on the Gun pit and during this time the ammunition becom was completed.	
	12.9.16		3 N.C.O. 10 men left for 10 day course at Clark.	
	20.9.16		Captain Cowan went on leave and handed over to 2/Lt Nicholls.	

WAR DIARY
or
INTELLIGENCE SUMMARY.

(Erase heading not required.)

Army Form C. 2118.

Place	Date	Hour	Summary of Events and Information	Remarks and references to Appendices.
Sailly la Bourse	26	5.16	The pit was again intended, it appears, much in favor of enemy trench mortar. Several rounds were fired at enemy trench mortar in Jager Graben which was much on the left. Stick is enfiladed at this point & a register was found on the side. The pit had about moderately well except the following iron. The gun registered one round at the sand target on several occasions afterwards. Position the gun is not fine afterwards under Repairs.	
	27	9.16		
	28	8.16		
	29	9.16		
	30	5.16		

J. A. Nickalls, Lt.
pro Capt Cmdg. V/ IIIrd HT.M.
26/5/16

8th, Division.

V/8, Heavy T? M. Battery.

October, 1916.

Army Form C. 2118.

WAR DIARY
or
INTELLIGENCE SUMMARY.
(Erase heading not required.)

Confidential

War Diary
of
V/8 Heavy Trench Mortar Battery.

From 1/10/16 ------ 31/10/16

Volume II

Place	Date	Hour	Summary of Events and Information	Remarks and references to Appendices

Army Form C. 2118.

WAR DIARY
or
INTELLIGENCE SUMMARY.
(Erase heading not required.)

Instructions regarding War Diaries and Intelligence Summaries are contained in F. S. Regs., Part II. and the Staff Manual respectively. Title pages will be prepared in manuscript.

Place	Date	Hour	Summary of Events and Information	Remarks and references to Appendices
In the Field	1 - 10/16		V/s. Heavy French Motor Battery was out of action (?) under repair from 1/10/16 – 8/10/16.	
	8/10 1 - 7/16		The gun commenced firing and continued to fire every day on an average of 15 rounds a day until the 21st instant.	
	6 - 10/16, 10/16		During this period the gun position was never located by the enemy. The gun's own chief objective was the series of enemy mortar positions of Jaeger French. These ultimately ceased firing and is due to absence.	
	8/16 1 - 7/16		Lts. Wray attended anti-gun course	
	21 - 7/16		2/Lt. T.A. Nichalls was attached 15 W/8 for duty with Stokes gun.	
	16 - 9/16		" " " " with Cauldron guns 16/10/16 – 21/10/16.	
	21 - 9/16		Lt. Tickard a.a. were attd. 15 V/8 for duty with Stokes gun.	
	11 - 9/16		" Carter D.a.V.	
	14 - 9/16		2/Lt. Large C.J. was admitted to Hospital	
	21 - 9/16		The Battery withdrew from action on handing over 15 & 21 Divs. at T.M. Bty.	
	22 - 11/16		The Battery left B. Saulty, le Bovure, proceeding South by train.	

WAR DIARY
or
INTELLIGENCE SUMMARY.

(Erase heading not required.)

Army Form C. 2118.

Place	Date	Hour	Summary of Events and Information	Remarks and references to Appendices
Sheffield	27/10/16	—	The Battery detrained at Edgehill Station and marched to the Citadel arriving at 3 AM 28/10/16.	
	28/10/16		The Btty was still out of the line	
	30/10/16		and on fatigues from div Artillery.	

J.H. Gorman Capt
V/8. HT.M. B.T.y.

8th, Division.

V/8, Heavy T. M. Battery.

November, 1916.

Army Form C. 2118.

WAR DIARY
or
INTELLIGENCE SUMMARY.
(Erase heading not required.)

Confidential

War Diary
of
V/8 Heavy Trench Mortar Battery

Jan 1/16 — 23/11/16

Volume III

Army Form C. 2118.

WAR DIARY
or
INTELLIGENCE SUMMARY.
(Erase heading not required.)

Place	Date	Hour	Summary of Events and Information	Remarks and references to Appendices
In the Field	1.11.16		1/8 Battery were sent out with a party from the clerks to 23rd Nov. 1915. the ground in front of the redoubt. Turning out under the supervision of the 6 Division. The Battery started to erect one Heavy Battery being attached to each Division, & the purpose, together the establishment of an Heavy Battery Reserve Supernumerary.	
	23.11.16			

J. E. Brown Capt
7c 1/8 H.T.R.Cty

8th Div.
I.Corps.

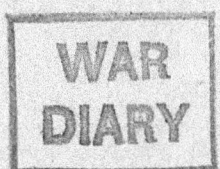

W/8 HEAVY TRENCH MORTAR BATTERY.

5th June 1916 to 5th August 1916.

WAR DIARY or INTELLIGENCE SUMMARY

Army Form C. 2118.

6/W/8 H.T.M. Batty.

Vol 1 - 2 + 3

Place	Date	Hour	Summary of Events and Information	Remarks and references to Appendices
ALBERT	5/5/16		Battery returned from 2nd Army report of work after the month of May.	
	6/5/16 to 25/5/16		Battery engaged in constructing two emplacements with ammunition pits therefore and tunnel entrances from trench and in making afresh two new emplacements connected with large ammunition recess in between. For the common use of both emplacements. Average depth of ammunition recess 20 feet, depth of under emplacements 12 feet. The bulk of this work being to burrow at that level and having (eg.) Army each the cuttings being roofed again with same 6" but of the cut earth supported below by corrugated iron, with 1st and logs. Estimate of earth cut and removed purely in said logs during this period 350 to 400 tons. Estimate of materials carried by hand lorry entrance to communication trench to captain of the bank 40 tons. Battery suffered no casualty during this period. Position of emplacements = Just on N. side of what a period full trench leading right handed off Rivington trench and two new trench leading left handed off Rivington st. Each emplacement being some 40 to 50 yds apart. The whole being opposite OVILLERS, the target allotted to the battery.	It includes 2 two mortars and 1500 rds

2449 Wt. W14957/Mg0 750,000 1/16 J.B.C. & A. Forms/C.2118/12.

WAR DIARY
or
INTELLIGENCE SUMMARY

Army Form C. 2118.

Place	Date	Hour	Summary of Events and Information	Remarks and references to Appendices
ALBERT	24/6/16		Artillery bombardment commenced.	
	26/6/16		Orders received from D.T.M.O. 8th Divn to take over two 9.45 Heavy Trench Mortars at Tramway Base near Chimney, ALBERT, with beds and equipment things, load them on to Tram cars and if possible get them into Trenches that night.	
		11.30pm	Commenced off loading from lorries and breaking up crates in which Mortars were packed. Progress slow owing to darkness rain and difficulty of carrying heights some 50/100 yds to cars, to which lorries could not approach.	
	27/6/16	2.30am	Mortars loaded on Cars. Communicated with 8. Divn. D.T.M.O. with difficulty owing to telephone having been cut by shellfire. Not right & received instructions not to take up Mortars that night.	
		9.30pm	Orders received from DTMO 8th Division to take Mortars into trenches that night.	
			Left tramway base. Bombarded at best. Torrential rain.	
		11.0pm	Arrived trenches Junction of Canister and Bacon Sect. Here more portable parts were sent by hand round Trenches to Mortar Pits. The three heavy parts of each Mortar (the piece revolving plate and bed) were pushed by hand to dead end in Tramway Cutting, thence by	

WAR DIARY
or
INTELLIGENCE SUMMARY
(Erase heading not required.)

Army Form C. 2118.

Place	Date	Hour	Summary of Events and Information	Remarks and references to Appendices
ALBERT	27/6/16		were to be carried by hand to Mitchell Street.	
		11.30pm to 3.30pm	This period of time was occupied in getting heavy trench mortar ammunition into the emplacements. The difficulties of carrying out the work being without doubt very great, and often entailing existing out the time were well nigh insuperable.	
	29/6/16	3.30pm to 5.30am	Occupied in clearing mortars and setting up some in situ.	
		5.30am	Commenced firing.	
		6.00am	Ceased firing.	
		7.30am	Commenced firing, heavy mist obliterated all observation.	
		8.0am	Ceased firing, as soon as we were instructed to fire as opportunity first offered, taking advantage of weather and other cover. During this period 60 Newton fell happy fired at varying intervals, the object being S.2. In afternoon of 30th a number of rounds fired at mid-his emplacement.	
	29/6/16 30/6/16 1/7/16	6.30am	Notley/mid in whence bombardment previous to infantry attack a.m. - 30. A fresh burst of intensified overhead burst of the previous rate was two Cenathes gave to a short hit on an emplacement.	
	2/7/16	3.30pm	Notley mid in intense bombardment previous to second infantry attack.	

WAR DIARY
or
INTELLIGENCE SUMMARY

Army Form C. 2118.

Place	Date	Hour	Summary of Events and Information	Remarks and references to Appendices
ALBERT	3/7/16	12.30 p.m.	Battery formed up to renew its attack and was only enabled by time 26 to change trail when not in action in the churned ammunition areas between nos 3 & 4 pits. During my my received two waggons out of four. During this period Battery fired 110 rounds, but nevertheless simply with work truck the Church* men and other support required clearing each and after informing to weather conditions and concussion & discharge. He writers were always pulling in. This greatly delighted matters and there were not been time to relief between firing, free time in which to work had to be done. At 12.15 we had orders to fire English charges the shrapnel with English but the heavy French English charges and ammunition generally were most unreliable and resulted in dangerously short fuses and misfires. On 30th we received orders to change to French charges. The time fuse of the English shrapnel is often to great criticism, considering the unreliability of the English charges. Our fire replied at times in ever increasing intensity & German pieces being brought up with intense count by the light. A time of enemy light shells and heavily about a ammunition depot was also struck. The Battery guns pieces were subject to rainy enemy shelling during the whole period.	* About about 450 +

'2449 Wt. W14957/M90 750,000 1/16 J.B.C. & A. Forms/C.2118/12.

Place	Date	Hour	Summary of Events and Information	Remarks and references to Appendices
ALBERT	1/7/16	3.0 am	Battery fired intense bombardment previous to attack by 12" & 6in which Battery was engaged. Fire continued for 2½ hours and 37 Yards were fired. Brig Rly Div opened in reply. The second fire was taken at rate of 50 rounds or 10 rounds per minute per Arm.	
	1/7/16	5.0 am	Orders received from DTMO 12th Division to take a Bank route from Tramway Nth & Chuinny ALBERT & then into 30 Eighth Avenue and change Range. Fire pole into old front German line on VILLERS how occupied by us and close own position, and fire on works at far side of Church about were a well up GOWERS POST by Tramway that dug it.	
	1/7/16		Position reconnoitred and ranges brought down read by head. Set up in shell hole just outside our then front line and short communication trench dug to road. Observation at 4 hrs of Arm rounds fired at 700 yards on a map range of 1500 two were rather short, one burst in air and one in own own infantry lines without known any casualties eventually received orders	
	6.30 pm		Ceased firing in Emergence and subsequently received orders from Division to deliver further no of English Ammun Arm.	

Army Form C. 2118.

WAR DIARY
or
INTELLIGENCE SUMMARY
(Erase heading not required.)

Instructions regarding War Diaries and Intelligence Summaries are contained in F. S. Regs., Part II. and the Staff Manual respectively. Title Pages will be prepared in manuscript.

Place	Date	Hour	Summary of Events and Information	Remarks and references to Appendices
ALBERT	15/7/16		Received orders this morning to push troops in Quicken Flour Post at big left hand curve in Trench Railway line, after clearing bits there are there.	
	18/7/16		Reworked ground in front of Quarry Post with a view to taking up entire line to Ferrar, thereby bringing in enemy lines. Owing to absence of cover and unreliability of ground it was found to be impracticable.	
	20/7/16		Battery was attached to 48th Division and worked in conjunction with that Division H.T.M. Batty, who had Officers hit. Lasted from mid. Two watery men extracting shrapnel for the far side of the Church in our lines. All operations were conducted by 48th H.T.M Batty Officers.	
	24/7/16		Natterys two Mortars in Mitchell Street were issued over to 25th Division who withdrew same.	
CROWN	29/7/16		Battery withdrew here with 48 Div Arty and subsequently joined	
	5/8/16		8th Division in BETHUNE area where it was disbanded.	

WAR DIARY
or
INTELLIGENCE SUMMARY

(Erase heading not required.)

Army Form C. 2118.

Instructions regarding War Diaries and Intelligence Summaries are contained in F. S. Regs., Part II. and the Staff Manual respectively. Title Pages will be prepared in manuscript.

Place	Date	Hour	Summary of Events and Information	Remarks and references to Appendices
On of Such			English ammunition was used in rifles taken from French & English prisoners. Telephone equipment of 2 reds and O.P. extremely inadequate. Few metallic circuits to fun. Pits and O.P. extremely inadequate. Transport of they chefs to 66 men and guns as in this very long with equipment and six tons extremely inadequate. With continuous firing and in not weather the walls of an emplacement unfold in being destroyed. One under bed of very heavy howitzer in few out 3 × 3 supporting the wooden handles of the wooden effectively prevented any sinking of the bed. At long range guns according to those caused by monster shoot was not attained. by French Ammunition. Lowest elevation fired at 47°. Ammunition pits close to by mail to avoid short turns in supply of ammunition to gun emplacement.	

1 2449   Wt. W14957/M90   750,000   1/16   J.B.C. & A.   Forms/C.2118/12.

WAR DIARY or INTELLIGENCE SUMMARY

Army Form C. 2118.

Place	Date	Hour	Summary of Events and Information	Remarks and references to Appendices
			N.C.O's and Strength of Battery 66 men + 1 subaltern. 1 Captain. Suggested that a Trench Mortar Battery should not be compared and solidarity of the "teachings" of other units, it being in this case to some extent experimental, the N.C.O's and men should at least be up to the average standard of efficiency and ability.	× Lieut Dawson W/S May 30 and taken over by Lieut Howes for R.A.
			Battery Confind chiefly of R.F.A. with few R.G.A. and six R.H.A. 1 Sergeant Major 1 Sergeant 10/12 Corporals & Bombardiers. J.W. Hoffman Capt R.F.A 9/c W/84 T.M.B.	

8th, Division.

Y/8, Medium T. M. Battery.

September, 1916.

CONFIDENTIAL.

8th DIVISIONAL ARTILLERY.

WAR DIARY

OF

Y/8. Medium Trench Mortar Bty

From 1-9-16 To 30-9-16.

(VOLUME 1)

With APPENDICES Nos. None.

Army Form C2118.

WAR DIARY
or
INTELLIGENCE SUMMARY. 1/Y/8 TMB

(Erase heading not required.)

Place	Date	Hour	Summary of Events and Information	Remarks and references to Appendices
2 Guns in action at than from our W.O.B.1 near Bate Adinfer Wood in Left Bayou Hohenzollern Sector.	1.9.16	3.30 p.m.	Casualties nil Ammunition expended 45 rds. Tactical Report 14 rds. fired at Gren Trench during afternoon 3 – 3.30 p.m. 31 rds. fired in Co-operation with STOKES on LITTLE WILLIE G4b ½ 4½ & G4b 4½. 7½ Many direct hits on parapet. No Enemy retaliation.	Report made by Lt Parkman, O.C. Y/8 TMB

WAR DIARY or INTELLIGENCE SUMMARY. Y/8 T.M.B.

Army Form C. 2118.

Place	Date	Hour	Summary of Events and Information	Remarks and references to Appendices
Hebuterne Sector	2.9.16		Leavillers rd. Ammunition expended 60 rounds. 60 rounds were fired at CROSS TRENCH and LITTLE WILLIE to harass enemy and destroy his trenches. A fair amount of enemy artillery and mortar fire was drawn from between 8 & twelve noon today. COMPONENT PARTS with reference to component parts many have come up to the Guns now and pact are generally deficient of fuzes. Ten containing S.A.A. Cartridges in many cases only contain three Cartridges instead of ten. (Ten sent with this record) 9 now require urgently 1 box component parts complete. 1 Tail 90 Cartridges SA 4 Fuzes Newton Ret by Lt Packman OC Y/8 TMB

Army Form C. 2118.

WAR DIARY
or
INTELLIGENCE SUMMARY. 1/8/718

(Erase heading not required.)

Place	Date	Hour	Summary of Events and Information	Remarks and references to Appendices.
To St Tilma	2.9.16		Following + return + D.A.C. on 4th inst.	
			Br. Colling.	
			L. Roots	
			" Clarke	
			" McMahon	
			" Dodd	
			" Johnson	
			" Chittenden	
				By Lt Parkman H. Comdg 4/1 8TMB.

Army Form C. 2118.

WAR DIARY
or
INTELLIGENCE SUMMARY.   /8 MB

(Erase heading not required.)

Place	Date	Hour	Summary of Events and Information	Remarks and references to Appendices
Hebuterne SK4	3.9.16		Demolition at Amm. Defended 24.	
Gun G in Cornwall RA.			Tactical Report Gun G fired 3 rounds in dart bearing LITTLE WILLIE. No more rounds have been fired during night.	
Gun F in Leff(Boyau)			Fired 31 rds. Observer and Endeavouring to locate heavy minenwerfer in HOGS BACK CRATER. There are probably two emplacement. Very heavy retaliation was brought upon us by our firing and about	
		11:30 am	Four heavy minenwerfer were firing PA 2.30 pm By Lt Pickhan OC Y/104	

2353 Wt. W2544/1454 700,000 5/15 D. D. & L.   A.D.S.S./Forms/C 2118.

Army Form C. 2118.

WAR DIARY
or
INTELLIGENCE SUMMARY.

Y/8 T.M.B.

(Erase heading not required.)

Instructions regarding War Diaries and Intelligence Summaries are contained in F. S. Regs., Part II. and the Staff Manual respectively. Title pages will be prepared in manuscript.

Place	Date	Hour	Summary of Events and Information	Remarks and references to Appendices
Hohenzollern Sector	4/9/16		Casualties nil. Ammunition expended 30.	
E Gun Off Bart Alley (in OB1)			TACTICAL REPORT 10 rds. were fired at CROSS TRENCH during 24 hours for offensive and destruction of enemy trench.	
F gun in Left Bogen Gun off Murray Alley		3-4 pm	Out of action, rifle mechanism etc. 20 rds. were fired at LITTLE WILLIE between 3 and 4 pm for destruction of enemy front line + wire.	
			Copy of Report for 5.9.16 sent K have been cut. C.E. By Lt Packman O.C. Y/8 T.M.B	

2353 Wt. W2544/1454 700,000 5/15 D. D. & L. A.D.S.S. Forms/C. 2118.

Army Form C. 2118.

WAR DIARY
or
INTELLIGENCE SUMMARY   Y/8 TMB

(Erase heading not required.)

Place	Date	Hour	Summary of Events and Information	Remarks and references to Appendices
Hollybrook Sector	6/9/16		Eighteen pounds fired since noon yesterday Casualties nil.	
E gun in O.Ps.			6 gun fired 8 rds — also few Shrapnel. At this period little firing was done in all the rear were working hard on dug-outs	Oliver Um 2Lt RFA Y/8 TMB

2449 Wt. W14957/M90 750,000 1/16 J.B.C. & A. Forms/C.2118/12.

Army Form C. 2118.

WAR DIARY
or
INTELLIGENCE SUMMARY 1/8 M.B

(Erase heading not required.)

Instructions regarding War Diaries and Intelligence Summaries are contained in F. S. Regs., Part II. and the Staff Manual respectively. Title Pages will be prepared in manuscript.

Place	Date	Hour	Summary of Events and Information	Remarks and references to Appendices
HOHENZOLLERN SECTOR	7.9.16		Number of rounds fired per yesterday now 35. Chief target — HOGS BACK (CRATER). At this time we were unable to reach the actual crater as we were not able to traverse left enough. Casualties nil.	C. An. 1/8 M.B

Army Form C. 2118.

WAR DIARY
or
INTELLIGENCE SUMMARY Y/8 TMB

(Erase heading not required.)

Place	Date	Hour	Summary of Events and Information	Remarks and references to Appendices
	8.9.16		Rounds fired since noon yesterday 24, thirteen during the firing last night. Our guns fired during the morning & night until the Boche ceased. CASUALTIES Nil. Some short bursts reported from E Gun, Palmato du & Sentry covert.	

C. Stu 2/LtRFA Y/8RFA

Army Form C. 2118.

● WAR DIARY
or
● INTELLIGENCE SUMMARY Y/8 TMB

(Erase heading not required.)

Instructions regarding War Diaries and Intelligence Summaries are contained in F. S. Regs., Part II. and the Staff Manual respectively. Title Pages will be prepared in manuscript.

Place	Date	Hour	Summary of Events and Information	Remarks and references to Appendices
HOHENZOLLERN SECTOR	9.9.16	12 noon	Casualty Report - nil from noon yesterday till noon today. Ammunition Expended - 10Y. TACTICAL REPORT E, F + G gun fired 10 rds. each on H098 BACK and	
E in O.B.1. off Bail. Alley F in Left Boyau G in Grenade Rd off Quarry Alley		2.20 am	LITTLE WILLIE in Co-operation with the Stokes mortars. F and G guns fired 30 and 28 rounds respectively for barrage fires on right and left of raiding party in retaliation and registration. 19 rounds fired in the afternoon. Lt. Packman was shot while observing fire. He died almost instantaneously. Cpl. Glendenning was with him and was slightly wounded, the bullet grazing his neck.	By Lt. Packman O.C. Y/8 T.M.B.

2449 Wt. W14957/M90 750,000 1/16 J.B.C. & A. Forms/C.2118/12.

Army Form C. 2118.

WAR DIARY
or
INTELLIGENCE SUMMARY

(Erase heading not required.)

Place	Date	Hour	Summary of Events and Information	Remarks and references to Appendices
HOHENZOLLERN SECTOR	10.9.16		Rounds fired prev. noon yesterday over 23. Lt. Packman was buried in the new portion of Vermelles Military Cemetery and a wooden cross erected on his grave. C.M. 4th R.R. 3/8 R.R.	

WAR DIARY
INTELLIGENCE SUMMARY

Y/8 T.M.B.

Place	Date	Hour	Summary of Events and Information	Remarks and references to Appendices
HOHENZOLLERN SECTOR	11.9.16		60 rounds fired in Co-operation with the Stokes since yesterday. Our fire was mainly offensive. The chief targets were LITTLE WILLIE and the Dumps second line. CASUALTIES NIL	Le Sein 2/Lt REA Y/8 T.M.B.

Army Form C. 2118.

WAR DIARY
or
INTELLIGENCE SUMMARY   Y/8 T.M.B.
(Erase heading not required.)

Place	Date	Hour	Summary of Events and Information	Remarks and references to Appendices
Aveluy Redoubt	12.9.16		60 rds. fired since noon yesterday. Chief targets same as passed — German support line. This day about noon one of our guns was buried with its detachment of 2 men — Gn. Hall and Hamblin. Both men were taken out alive with the help of some prisoners and were taken to F.A. Station.	

e. Salt /Lieut
OC Y/VIII TMB

Army Form C. 2118.

WAR DIARY
or
INTELLIGENCE SUMMARY
(Erase heading not required.)

Place	Date	Hour	Summary of Events and Information	Remarks and references to Appendices
Hohenzollern Sector	13.9.16		Rounds fired since yesterday nov 14. Chief Target HINDENBURG & FOSSE TRENCHES. It is only possible to fire by map at the German second line on this sector as observation is impossible owing to the nature of the ground. CASUALTIES NIL.	Will HARRIS Capt. O.C. 91/8 Bde.

WAR DIARY or **INTELLIGENCE SUMMARY** Y/1 & T.M.B.

Army Form C. 2118.

Place	Date	Hour	Summary of Events and Information	Remarks and references to Appendices
Achurydom Redoubt	14.9.16		Rounds fired during Yesterday noon #4. Abul tayet - Heavy minenwerfer opposite left of our front. One oilcan was reported silenced.	Y/1 & T.M.B. 2o Sew Lt R.F.H. O.C. Y/1 & T.M.B.

Army Form C. 2118.

WAR DIARY
or
INTELLIGENCE SUMMARY   Y/8 TMB
(Erase heading not required.)

Place	Date	Hour	Summary of Events and Information	Remarks and references to Appendices
Kemmel Sector	15.9.16		Rounds fired on 14 Yesterday nine. The expenditure of ammunition was due to small expenditure of ammunition was due to a desire to gain as much as possible at that particular time. The detachments were also partially employed making supports and head-cover. C. Ellis % 1st RFA OC Y/8 TMB	

Place	Date	Hour	Summary of Events and Information	Remarks and references to Appendices
Khuzdar Sector	16.9.16		Casualties nil. Rounds fired since yesterday 38. A steady rate of fire was kept up during three days. Also many shots were daily arranged in conjunction with Stokes. One noticed that the stokes motar generally finished a good while before ours. Perhaps a time limit might be arranged for both.	

A. Sim ?/RFA
OC ?/?MB

Army Form C. 2118.

● WAR DIARY
or
● INTELLIGENCE SUMMARY 7/8 TMB

(Erase heading not required.)

Instructions regarding War Diaries and Intelligence Summaries are contained in F. S. Regs., Part II. and the Staff Manual respectively. Title Pages will be prepared in manuscript.

Place	Date	Hour	Summary of Events and Information	Remarks and references to Appendices
Ashun Allam Cuts	14.9.16		Rounds fired 53. Report by 2/Lt Silvester. A large number of rounds were gradually being accumulated at guns. On this day there were 334 ( ). On 15th there were 404. J. S.	

WAR DIARY
or
INTELLIGENCE SUMMARY

Army Form C. 2118.

Y/8 T.M.B.

Place	Date	Hour	Summary of Events and Information	Remarks and references to Appendices
Holeuzelle Sector	15.9.16		Rounds fired 50. A steady rate of fire. Casualties nil.	

WAR DIARY
or
INTELLIGENCE SUMMARY   H/Q M.B.

Army Form C. 2118.

Place	Date	Hour	Summary of Events and Information	Remarks and references to Appendices
Hamilton Cuts	19.9.16		Rounds fired 51. Casualties nil. Tactical porpoises shoot by 2/Lt. Stewart — "Shelled CROSS TRENCH and Communication Trench leading thereto with 20 rds. with successful results judging by amount of material thrown up. Also shelled LITTLE WILLIE and HINDENBURG TRENCH and afterwards with good results — to the extent of thirty rounds."	e. Sely 1st RCA O/C 4th R.T.M.B.

WAR DIARY or INTELLIGENCE SUMMARY

Army Form C. 2118.

Place	Date	Hour	Summary of Events and Information	Remarks and references to Appendices
Martinpuich	20.9.16		Casualties nil. Rounds fired 28. Tactical proposition report of Lt Gibson — "H.M.LS. Shellas LITTLE WILLIE + HINDENBURG TRENCHES with 28 rds. Can say considerable approach being watched 150 - per. the did not damage being in the Normans at all." C.E.	

WAR DIARY

INTELLIGENCE SUMMARY Y/8 TMB

Army Form C. 2118.

Place	Date	Hour	Summary of Events and Information	Remarks and references to Appendices
Hohenzollern Sector	21.9.16		No. 9 ldr. force A.G. Casualties nil. Tactical report by Lt Liberski:— "Yellow LITTLE WILLIE from G.4.b.4.4. to Sub.St. 6½ causing great damage portion by trench stc blown up. Gun pits were blown up which crossed Comm. trench at G.4.b.43.68. and G.4.b.50.25 making it possible to see down these Comm. trenches for about 50 yds." C.S.	

Army Form C. 2118.

WAR DIARY
or
INTELLIGENCE SUMMARY

(Erase heading not required.)

Place	Date	Hour	Summary of Events and Information	Remarks and references to Appendices
Anzibn Suite	27.9.16		Cas. Nil. Rds. fired 40. Tactical Reports by 2/Lt Silverston :—	
		5.30 p.m	"5.30 p.m. we fired 32 rds pct. 94d 42.4 & 94f 32.6½. LITTLE WILLIE. About 30 yds of trench & wire were completely destroyed. There dugouts were blown up & a snipers post. The damage was similar — the whole parapet being breached, dates loaded wire, & gun emplmnts — guns were he fired 8 more with direct hits on the Minenwerfer trench." C.S.	

WAR DIARY
or
INTELLIGENCE SUMMARY

4/5 MGB

Army Form C. 2118.

Place	Date	Hour	Summary of Events and Information	Remarks and references to Appendices
Holnon Sectr	23.8. 16		Rounds fired 21. Tactical report of 11 Silvester "filled Hindenburg Trench + approaches with 21 rds. Satisfactory results were obtained" e.S.	

WAR DIARY
INTELLIGENCE SUMMARY

Place	Date	Hour	Summary of Events and Information	Remarks and references to Appendices
Aubigny sur Ton	24.9.16		Cas. nil. Res. feed +1. Tactical report During ucping a continuous T.M. dual took place G.M. Opr RFA OC Y/8 TMB	

WAR DIARY
INTELLIGENCE SUMMARY

Place	Date	Hour	Summary of Events and Information	Remarks and references to Appendices
Holnon pertes	25/9/18		Rds fired 102. Casualties nil. Tactical report. Intense artillery of T.M. & from 7.30 am till 11.30 a.m.	

e. Mi, Lt RFA
OC. X/e TMB

Army Form C. 2118.

WAR DIARY
or
INTELLIGENCE SUMMARY Y/8 T.M.B.
(Erase heading not required.)

Place	Date	Hour	Summary of Events and Information	Remarks and references to Appendices
Kingthorn Craters	26.5.16		Rds. fired 80 Cas. nil. Tactical report:- Heavy T.M. fighting once I am. Enemy secured line to fired continuously, having different positions.	

Army Form C. 2118.

WAR DIARY
or
INTELLIGENCE SUMMARY 4/16 MB

(Erase heading not required.)

Place	Date	Hour	Summary of Events and Information	Remarks and references to Appendices
Hénuplu Sector	29/4/16		Rds fired 48. Tactical Report:- Hi enemy. Enemy began to strafe at 7.30 am. We immediately put in 84 rounds in reply. Fw.5 oil cans. Oil cans have come from Hot's BACK CRATER. Enemy has scarcely fired even. Cas. nil. C. M. 7/RHA	4/16 MB

Army Form C. 2118.

WAR DIARY
or
INTELLIGENCE SUMMARY

(Erase heading not required.) 1/6 M.B.

Place	Date	Hour	Summary of Events and Information	Remarks and references to Appendices
Hohenzollern Sector	28.9.16		Cas. nil. B[attalio]n fired on a Yesterday 68. In addition we fired about 15 rifle rnds - sent up at 11.50 - & to be included in report for 29th.) Tac. R.F.A. We laid a gun on Gun in the command in the afternoon fire but as he commenced silenced him for We sent over 23 and have been at the time. We must have been on around his actual position as far as we Cras Drawn from our Craters. lightly placed. Infantry E. Ellis 9th R.F.	

8th, Division.

Y/8, Medium T. M. Battery.

October, 1916.

Army Form C. 2118.

WAR DIARY
or
INTELLIGENCE SUMMARY.
(Erase heading not required.)

CONFIDENTIAL

War Diary
of
Y/8 Medium Trench Mortar Battery

From 1.10.16 to 31.10.16.

Volume II.

Army Form C. 2118.

WAR DIARY
or
INTELLIGENCE SUMMARY.
(Erase heading not required.)

Instructions regarding War Diaries and Intelligence Summaries are contained in F. S. Regs., Part II. and the Staff Manual respectively. Title pages will be prepared in manuscript.

Place	Date	Hour	Summary of Events and Information	Remarks and references to Appendices
HOHENZOLLERN SECTOR	1.10.16		Ammn. Report Rounds fired 69. Casualties Nil. Tactical: HINDENBURGH TRENCH, LITTLE WILLIE and HOG'S BACK CRATER were shelled during the 24 hrs. Sunday - noon 1.10.16. Otherwise trenches on our front & support lines.	
"	2.10.16		Ammn. Report Rounds fired 51. Casualties Nil. Tactical Report HOG'S BACK CRATER, where enemy has been busy for last few days, has been shelled. Our enemy front & support lines (Hindenburgh & Little Willie) where enemy tried to mount some bridges. 30 who were found during night.	

Army Form C. 2118.

WAR DIARY
or
INTELLIGENCE SUMMARY.
(Erase heading not required.)

Instructions regarding War Diaries and Intelligence Summaries are contained in F. S. Regs., Part II. and the Staff Manual respectively. Title pages will be prepared in manuscript.

Place	Date	Hour	Summary of Events and Information	Remarks and references to Appendices
HOHENZOLLERN REDOUBT.	3.10.16		10 rounds fired on G.4.B.6.5. Operation Offensive. Burst damage to enemy's defences. Rapid fire on HOG'S BACK at times given by Division (for 5 minutes each.) Enemy retaliated on QUARRY ALLEY. Trench mortars silenced. Rounds fired 43. Casualties nil.	
	4.10.16		Good shooting done at minenwerfer G.4.B.7.6.6.½. Rounds fired 25. Casualties nil.	
	5.10.16		Shelled enemy's communication trenches & front line at 2.45pm & 10.45p. Enemy's retaliation feeble, but his shooting was good. Rounds fired 26. Casualty 2nd Lt Ellis wounded.	
	6.10.16		CROSS TRENCH, HINDENBERG & LITTLE WILLIE shelled. HINDENBERG & approaches fired on according to Divisional programme. Rounds fired 262. Casualties nil.	
	7.10.16		Ran-jar at G.4.B.43.68 fired on two direct hits obtained. HOG'S BACK CRATER & LITTLE WILLIE shelled also minenwerfer at G.4.B.35.97. Rounds fired 60. Casualties nil.	
	8.10.16		Considerable damage observed as result of firing on HOG'S BACK. Toppled in LITTLE WILLIE fired on. Rounds fired 67. Casualties nil.	

Army Form C. 2118.

WAR DIARY
or
INTELLIGENCE SUMMARY.
(Erase heading not required.)

Instructions regarding War Diaries and Intelligence Summaries are contained in F. S. Regs., Part II. and the Staff Manual respectively. Title pages will be prepared in manuscript.

Place	Date	Hour.	Summary of Events and Information	Remarks and references to Appendices
HOHENZOLLERN REDOUBT.	9.10.16		Hog's Back craters fired on with much damage. Hindenburg Trench traversed & barbed tram up. Rounds fired 72. Casualties nil.	

WAR DIARY
or
INTELLIGENCE SUMMARY
(Erase heading not required.)

Army Form C. 2118.

Place	Date	Hour	Summary of Events and Information	Remarks and references to Appendices
Hohenzollern Redoubt	~~9.10.16~~		~~Reported into Bn. Hd Qrs. this day, as 2th Lt. on part as acting officer on account of shortage of~~ ~~Nedad~~ ~~officers~~ ~~Stanley~~ ~~Enemy were kept off the line~~	C.
"	10.10.16		Amm Report. Round fired 79. Casualties Nil. Tactical Report. Enemy front to rear been shelled. Enemy replied with heavy minenwerfer.	N/E
"	11.10.16		Firing was carried out during day on HOGS BACK and HINDENBURG TRENCH and on gaberg from new 94.4.72. AMM. REPORT by J Somers fired 51. CASUALTIES. NIL.	
"	12.10.16		Firing on HINDENBURG witch's back also on communication trench. Enemy retaliated with minenwerfer on LEFT BOYAU. 64 rounds fired. Casualties nil.	

Army Form C. 2118.

Instructions regarding War Diaries and Intelligence Summaries are contained in F.S. Regs., Part II. and the Staff Manual respectively. Title pages will be prepared in manuscript.

WAR DIARY
or
INTELLIGENCE SUMMARY.
(Erase heading not required.)

Place	Date	Hour	Summary of Events and Information	Remarks and references to Appendices
HOHENZOLLERN REDOUBT.	13.10.16		Firing carried out on CROSS TRENCH and HINDENBERG. Several direct hits observed. Enemy retaliated during night of 12/13th on MUD ALLEY, but guns were not touched. No. of rounds fired 64. Casualties nil.	
	14.10.16		Approaches to HINDENBERG trench from LITTLE WILLIE shelled. Firing carried out on HOG'S BACK CRATERS and HINDENBERG TRENCH. Enemy exceptionally quiet. No. of rounds fired 60. Casualties nil.	
	15.10.16		Bombardment of trenches from G.4.3.5.½ to G.4.3.5.3 according to Divisional programme. Much damage was observed as result of fire on HINDENBERG TRENCH. Enemy has several new mortars in line — light minenwerfer & light trench mortars. These have not been in action for some time. No. of rounds fired 81. Casualties nil.	
	16.10.16		Firing carried out on HINDENBERG trench & LITTLE WILLIE. During firing on HOG'S BACK CRATER a number of bombs was thrown up. Enemy has been exceptionally quiet for the last 24 hours. No. of rounds fired 46. Casualties nil.	

WAR DIARY
or
INTELLIGENCE SUMMARY
(Erase heading not required.)

Army Form C. 2118.

Place	Date	Hour	Summary of Events and Information	Remarks and references to Appendices
HOHENZOLLERN REDOUBT.	17.10.15		Gun positions improved during evening.	
		4:30 pm	Enemy started heavy bombardment and "Rum Jar" fire on our lines. Rifle fire immediately carried out in conjunction with Stokes' gun. Enemy silenced. Casualties nil. No of rounds fired 64.	
	19.10.16		Bombardment carried out in co-operation with Stokes' gun. Good shooting shown. About forty rounds were fired in retaliation to enemy's fire. Casualties nil. No of rounds fired 84.	
	19.10.16		Strafing carried out in conjunction with Stokes' gun. Direct hit on E gun position (LEFT BOYAU) 50 rounds blown up. Thereafter found would make a great gun position after a month or so. Casualties nil. No of rounds fired 38.	
	20.10.16		Combined firing of Stokes' & howitzers on LITTLE WILLIE & HINDENBURG. Results satisfactory. No of rounds fired 39. Casualties nil.	
	21.10.16		Firing carried out on HOG'S BACK & LITTLE WILLIE trench. Hits were observed. No of rounds fired 30. Casualty:- 15761. Pte BOWLER (R.BERKS) killed.	

WAR DIARY
~~INTELLIGENCE SUMMARY~~

Army Form C. 2118.

Place	Date	Hour	Summary of Events and Information	Remarks and references to Appendices
HOHENZOLLERN REDOUBT.	22.10.16		Relieved by 21st DIVISION Artillery. Trench Mortars.	
	23.10.16		Battery moved to CITADEL camp (near FRICOURT)	
	23.10.16 to 31.10.16		Battery in rest at CITADEL Camp.	

8th, Division.

Y/8, Medium T. M. Battery.

November, 1916.

Army Form C. 2118.

WAR DIARY
or
INTELLIGENCE SUMMARY.
(Erase heading not required.)

CONFIDENTIAL

WAR DIARY

Y/2 Medium Trench Mortar Battery

From 1.11.16   To 30.11.16

Volume III

Army Form C. 2118.

WAR DIARY
or
INTELLIGENCE SUMMARY
(Erase heading not required.)

Instructions regarding War Diaries and Intelligence Summaries are contained in F.S. Regs., Part II. and the Staff Manual respectively. Title pages will be prepared in manuscript.

Place	Date	Hour	Summary of Events and Information	Remarks and references to Appendices
CITADEL	1.11.16	9 am	On 1.11.16 the battery moved about 1 mile North East from the CITADEL. The move was done with hand-carts.	
Position a mile NE	2.11.16 3.11.16		Latrines were dug and bivouacs put-up.	
of CITADEL	4.11.16		One N.C.O. and 10 men were temporarily reported to No 2 Section 8th D.A.C.	
"	5.11.16		One N.C.O. and 3 men went on working party today on K.L. or ascent of long road. Returned same day.	
"	6.11.16		1 N.C.O and 2 men went on patrol to H.Q. 8th D.A.C. for work on patrols to be continued until further orders.	

Army Form C. 2118.

WAR DIARY
or
INTELLIGENCE SUMMARY.
(Erase heading not required.)

Instructions regarding War Diaries and Intelligence Summaries are contained in F. S. Regs., Part II. and the Staff Manual respectively. Title pages will be prepared in manuscript.

Place	Date	Hour	Summary of Events and Information	Remarks and references to Appendices
"MANSELL CAMP"	7.11.16 to		Battery training carried out with men available. Deficiencies of kit etc made up	
	12.11.16		Battery bivouack at F.17.c. ("Mansell Camp".)	R.O.W.
"	13.11.16		One NCO attached to 45th Bde. R.F.A.	
			6 men attached to "O" Batt. R.H.A.	R.O.W.
"	14.11.16 to 16.11.16		Care and cleaning of gun stores etc by NCOs and men remaining with battery.	R.O.W.
"	17.11.16		O.C. Batt. (2nd Lieut. GELLIS) attached to 3rd Batt. 45th Bde R.F.A.	
			2nd Lieut C.N. SILVESTER posted to "O" Batt. R.H.A.	R.O.W.
"	18.11.16		Attached men returned to Battery.	
			H.Q. Camps for MARICOURT	
			Horses forwarded	
	29.11.16 to 30.11.16			

8th, Division.

Y/8, Medium T. M. Battery.

December, 1916.

Army Form C. 2118.

WAR DIARY
or
INTELLIGENCE SUMMARY.
(Erase heading not required.)

CONFIDENTIAL.

WAR DIARY
of
Y/8 TRENCH MORTAR BATTERY.

from 1.12.16 to 31.12.16.

Volume III.

Army Form C. 2118.

WAR DIARY
or
INTELLIGENCE SUMMARY.
(Erase heading not required.)

Instructions regarding War Diaries and Intelligence Summaries are contained in F. S. Regs., Part II. and the Staff Manual respectively. Title pages will be prepared in manuscript.

Place	Date	Hour	Summary of Events and Information	Remarks and references to Appendices
Line of march	1.12.16		Line of march.	
ANDAINVILLE (SOMME)	2.12.16		Arrived at ANDAINVILLE (SOMME) Battery Billeted.	7.0p.m.
	9.12.16		Battery training carried out.	
LIOMER (SOMME)	16.12.16		Moved to LIOMER (SOMME) Battery Billeted.	2.0p.m.
	28.12.16		Battery training carried out. (Physical work drill etc)	
	29.12.16		Line of march.	3.0p.m.

8th, Division.

Z/8, Medium T. M. Battery.

September, 1916.

CONFIDENTIAL.

8th DIVISIONAL ARTILLERY.

WAR DIARY

OF

Z/8 Medium Trench Mortar Bty.

From 1-9-16 To 30-9-16

(VOLUME 1)

With APPENDICES Nos. None

Army Form C. 2118.

WAR DIARY
or
INTELLIGENCE=SUMMARY

(Erase heading not required.)

Z/5 Trench Mortar Battery

Place	Date	Hour	Summary of Events and Information	Remarks and references to Appendices
In the field	October 1916			
	1-14		Enemy front and support lines were continually bombarded at G.12.a.31. Where one T.M. and two M.G. were reported to be firing from. Enemy have since abandoned firing from the positions.	
	15-20		Enemy salient between points G.12.a.4.0 and G.12.a.6.0 were successfully bombarded. A Pram T.M. was compelled to change its position.	
	20-24		Wire was successfully cut on enemy front.	
	24-26		Enemy bombarded our lines for a period of seven hours each of the three days. Vigorous retaliation was made to his fire.	
	27-28		Bombarded the dug-outs round points G.12.a.2.4.? and completely silenced a 200 m/m T.M.	
	29		A working party of 5 belonging to 15/8 ?? caught by an aerial dart. Casualties resulting were One killed and four wounded	
	30		Completely knocked an enemy T.M. firing aerial darts.	

E.R.P. Brown 2/Lt
Z/18 T.M. Battery

8th, Division.

Z/8, MEDIUM T. M. Battery.

October, 1916.

Army Form C. 2118.

WAR DIARY
or
INTELLIGENCE SUMMARY
(Erase heading not required.)

Confidential

War Diary
of
Z.11/8 T.M. Battery
From Oct 1. to Oct 31st
1916
Volume II

Army Form C. 2118.

WAR DIARY
or
INTELLIGENCE SUMMARY

(Erase heading not required.)

Instructions regarding War Diaries and Intelligence Summaries are contained in F. S. Regs., Part II. and the Staff Manual respectively. Title Pages will be prepared in manuscript.

Place	Date	Hour	Summary of Events and Information	Remarks and references to Appendices
Quarries Sector	1/10/16		In conjunction with Stokes enemys front and support lines were bombarded between points G12a 4.0 and G12a 6.0.	
	2/10/16 to 5/10/16		In conjunction with Stokes and Artillery the 2" Mortars bombarded enemy's wire and front line. Wire between bayaux 77 and 79. On the night of the 5th/6th a raid by the Sherwoods was made and he found to have been completely destroyed by the 2" mortars. Over 700 rounds were fired by the battery during this period of four days.	
	6/10/16 to 10/10/16		Cooperating with Stokes enemys front & support lines were heavily bombarded. Enemy retaliation was weak; he fired on an average 20 H.T.M shells per diem.	

Army Form C. 2118.

Sheet II

WAR DIARY
or
INTELLIGENCE SUMMARY
(Erase heading not required.)

Instructions regarding War Diaries and Intelligence Summaries are contained in F. S. Regs., Part II. and the Staff Manual respectively. Title Pages will be prepared in manuscript.

Place	Date	Hour	Summary of Events and Information	Remarks and references to Appendices
	11/10/16 to 13/10/16		Over 200 rounds were fired on enemy's front line between bayonets 79 and 77. Patrols reported the day previous to 11/10/16 that the enemy wire twenty6 sending that sector of his front line which had been previously demolished by our fire. The enemy seemed to have established a large movement of Very light exploding out of the concealed on twelve Very light's were set on fire.	
	14/10/16 to 20/10/16		Co-operating with Stokes and rigators have lately ment of enemy's front ? communication and support trenches was made during this period between G.12.a.2.4. and G.12.a.6.0. Great damage appears to have been caused and in one place the enemy parapet was breached by our fire and the enemy snipers claim little direct hits.	

Army Form C. 2118.

WAR DIARY
or
INTELLIGENCE SUMMARY
(Erase heading not required.)

Sheet III

Place	Date	Hour	Summary of Events and Information	Remarks and references to Appendices
	21/10/16 to 22/10/16		No rifle firing was possible owing to mechanisms going out of action and ordnance being unable to replace them. There was a material scarcity of T. Tubes available.	
	22/10/16		2/Lt Ribby was recalled to 1st D.A.C. Lt Martin was appointed O.C. W/8 H.T. M.B. 2/Lt Brown was appointed O.C. 1st Battn (2/8). The battery came out of the line on handing over to 1st M.T.M's 1st Battn 21st Div.	
	23/10/16 24/10/16		The battery travelled by lorries to the Citadel. The battery demounted at the Citadel at rest. During the month the battery has retained its complete superiority of fire over the enemys T.M's. On an average 4.6" lots per diem were fired by the battery.	

G.R.P. Brown 2 Lieut R.F.A.
Commanding 2/8 Trench Mortar Battery

2/Lt E. Zilwa
2 Lieut R.F.A
31-10-16

8th, Division.

Z/8, Medium T. M. Battery.

November, 1916.

Army Form C. 2118.

WAR DIARY
or
INTELLIGENCE SUMMARY.
(Erase heading not required.)

Confidential

War Diary

Z/8 Trench Mortar Battery

Period November 1st to 31st 1916

Vol II

WAR DIARY
or
INTELLIGENCE SUMMARY.

Army Form C. 2118.

Place	Date	Hour	Summary of Events and Information	Remarks and references to Appendices
	1/11/16		Engaged on general fatigues at Ammunition Column and batteries of 8th & 15th Div's	
	30/11/16			

G.P.Bateson 2/Lt TFA
OC 2/8 T.M.B.

8th, Division.

Z/8, Medium T. M. Battery.

December, 1916.

Army Form C. 2118.

WAR DIARY
or
INTELLIGENCE SUMMARY

(Erase heading not required.)

Confidential

War Diary

Z/8 Trench Mortar Battery

December 1st 1916

to

December 31st 1916

Vol I

Army Form C. 2118.

WAR DIARY
or
INTELLIGENCE SUMMARY.
(Erase heading not required.)

Instructions regarding War Diaries and Intelligence Summaries are contained in F. S. Regs., Part II. and the Staff Manual respectively. Title pages will be prepared in manuscript.

Place	Date	Hour	Summary of Events and Information	Remarks and references to Appendices
	1/12/16 – 2/12/16		Battery on line of march	
	3/12/16 – 10/12/16		Battery in rest	
	10/12/16 – 29/12/16		Training period	
	29/12/16 – 31/12/16		Battery on line of march	

In The Field
31-12-1916

C.H.P. Howry, Lieut
O/c 7/8 Trench Mortar Battery

CONFIDENTIAL.

8th. DIVISIONAL ARTILLERY

WAR DIARY
OF
X.Y.Z.T.W/8 T.M. Batteries

From 1.1.17. To 31.1.17.

(VOLUME 4)

With Appendices Nos. None

Army Form C. 2118.

WAR DIARY
or
INTELLIGENCE SUMMARY.
(Erase heading not required.)

CONFIDENTIAL

WAR DIARY

OF

X/8 Medium Trench Mortar Battery

From 1-1-1917 To 31-1-1917.

VOL IV

Army Form C. 2118.

WAR DIARY
or
INTELLIGENCE SUMMARY.
(Erase heading not required.)

Place	Date	Hour	Summary of Events and Information	Remarks and references to Appendices
In the Field	January Feb 16 18th		The Battery was employed in training and General Fatigues.	
	Jan 19th to 31st		The Battery attended a Course of Instruction at Fourth Army School of Mortars	

Newman
Capt.
O.T.M.O. 8th Dn R.A.
fr O.C. T/R T.M.B.

Army Form C. 2118.

WAR DIARY
or
INTELLIGENCE SUMMARY.
(Erase heading not required.)

CONFIDENTIAL

WAR DIARY
of
Y/8 Medium Trench Mortar Battery

From 1.1.17 to 31.1.17

VOLUME IV

Army Form C. 2118.

WAR DIARY
or
INTELLIGENCE SUMMARY.
(Erase heading not required.)

Instructions regarding War Diaries and Intelligence Summaries are contained in F.S. Regs., Part II. and the Staff Manual respectively. Title pages will be prepared in manuscript.

Place	Date	Hour	Summary of Events and Information	Remarks and references to Appendices
	1-1-17		Marched from Camp 14 to MAR ICOURT for 6 days. E.E.	
	11-1-17		Returned to rest-billets at VAUX SUR SOMME. E.E.	
	27-1-17		Left VAUX-SUR-SOMME and went to Camp 17. E.E.	

Army Form C. 2118.

WAR DIARY
or
INTELLIGENCE SUMMARY.
(Erase heading not required.)

Confidential
War Diary
of
Z/8 Trench Mortar Battery
From January 1st 1917.
To January 31st 1917

Vol IV

Army Form C. 2118.

WAR DIARY
or
INTELLIGENCE SUMMARY.
(Erase heading not required.)

Instructions regarding War Diaries and Intelligence Summaries are contained in F. S. Regs., Part II. and the Staff Manual respectively. Title pages will be prepared in manuscript.

Place	Date	Hour	Summary of Events and Information	Remarks and references to Appendices
	January 1st to 31st		The Battery was employed in training and General fatigues.	

for O/c 2/8 Th Battery
Gunner A. Fletcher 2y/4.

Army Form C. 2118.

WAR DIARY
or
INTELLIGENCE SUMMARY.
(Erase heading not required.)

— Confidential —

War Diary
of
W/8 Heavy Trench Mortar Battery
From 1.1.1917 To 31.1.1917

Army Form C. 2118.

WAR DIARY
or
INTELLIGENCE SUMMARY.
(Erase heading not required.)

Instructions regarding War Diaries and Intelligence Summaries are contained in F. S. Regs., Part II. and the Staff Manual respectively. Title pages will be prepared in manuscript.

Place	Date	Hour	Summary of Events and Information	Remarks and references to Appendices
In a.	9(?) 10/5 9/7		Battery men not in action between the 9 & 15, employed on General Fatigues & in rest.	

Maurice Yeats
O.C ??? ?/?.?.?.?

T2134. Wt. W708—776. 500000. 4/15. Sir J. C. & S.

Army Form C. 2118.

WAR DIARY
or
INTELLIGENCE SUMMARY.
(Erase heading not required.)

CONFIDENTIAL

WAR DIARY
Y/5 Medium Trench Mortar Battery
From 1.1.17 to 31.11.17
VOLUME II

Army Form C. 2118.

WAR DIARY
or
INTELLIGENCE SUMMARY.
(Erase heading not required.)

Instructions regarding War Diaries and Intelligence Summaries are contained in F. S. Regs., Part II. and the Staff Manual respectively. Title pages will be prepared in manuscript.

Place	Date	Hour	Summary of Events and Information	Remarks and references to Appendices

Army Form C. 2118.

WAR DIARY
or
INTELLIGENCE SUMMARY.
(Erase heading not required.)

CONFIDENTIAL

WAR DIARY

of

X/8 T.M. BATT.

from 1.1.1917 to 31.1.1917.

Vol. II.

WAR DIARY
or
INTELLIGENCE SUMMARY.
(Erase heading not required.)

Army Form C. 2118.

Date	Hour	Summary of Events and Information	Remarks and references to Appendices
...COURT 1.1.17		Line of march from LIOMER-SUR-SOMME to MARICOURT.	8.0.m.
2.1.17		Fatigues for field batteries (mess, marking etc.)	8.0.m.
3.1.17			8.0.m.
VAUX (CORBIE) 11.1.17 to 11.1.17		Line of march from MARICOURT to next billets at VAUX (near CORBIE). Battery in rest at VAUX. 2/Lt SILVESTER attached 4/c Battery, S/Lt MERCER attached 4/c Battery.	8.0.m. 8.0.m.
VAUX-L'AMIENOIS 4.1.17 to 31.1.17		Battery attached 4th Army MORTAR SCHOOL. (VAUX-L'AMIENOIS) for instruction.	8.0.m.

Lieutenant 3/Lt.
4/50th Battn.

CONFIDENTIAL.

8th DIVISIONAL ARTILLERY.

WAR DIARY

OF

W.X.Y.Z. Trench Mortar Batteries

From 1st Feby 1917 To 28 Feby 1917

(VOLUME VI)

With APPENDICES Nos.

Army Form C. 2118.

WAR DIARY
or
INTELLIGENCE SUMMARY.
(Erase heading not required.)

Confidential

War — Diary
of
W/8 Heavy Trench Mortar Battery
From 1.2.17 to 28.2.17

Vol VI

WAR DIARY
or
INTELLIGENCE SUMMARY.

(Erase heading not required.)

Army Form C. 2118.

Place	Date	Hour	Summary of Events and Information	Remarks and references to Appendices
In the field	1.2.17 to 28/2/17		Battery employed building Observation Posts &c	

G Morris Capt
O Comdg 14/6 Hy A.K.B

Army Form C. 2118.

WAR DIARY
or
INTELLIGENCE SUMMARY.
(Erase heading not required.)

— Confidential —

War ———— Diary.

of

X/8 Medium Trench Mortar Battery

From 1. 2. 17 to 28. 2. 17

Vol VI

Army Form C. 2118.

WAR DIARY
or
INTELLIGENCE SUMMARY.
(Erase heading not required.)

Instructions regarding War Diaries and Intelligence Summaries are contained in F. S. Regs., Part II. and the Staff Manual respectively. Title pages will be prepared in manuscript.

Place	Date	Hour	Summary of Events and Information	Remarks and references to Appendices
In the Field	1/2/17 to 2/2/17		Awaiting transport from Fourth Army School of Mortars	¼ Gun
	3-3-17		VAUX-en-AMIENOIS.	
			Moved from School of Mortars to Camps 17. SUZANNE.	¼ Gun
	4-2-17 to 6-2-17		Billetted Camps 17.	¼ Gun
	7-2-17 to 11-2-17		N.C.O.'s and Men moved to Le Forest and engaged on R.A. Fatigues	¼ Gun
	11-2-17 to 28-2-17		Building emplacements for two Mortars	¼ Gun
				¼ Gun attd. 2nd Lt.
				for G.C. ¼ / ? T.M. Battery

Army Form C. 2118.

WAR DIARY
or
INTELLIGENCE SUMMARY.
(Erase heading not required.)

Confidential

War Diary

V/5 Medium Trench Mortar Battery

From 1.2.17 to 28.2.17

Vol VI

Army Form C. 2118.

WAR DIARY
or
INTELLIGENCE SUMMARY.
(Erase heading not required.)

Place	Date	Hour	Summary of Events and Information	Remarks and references to Appendices
In the Field	1.2.17 to 28.2.17		Battery employed building Observation post etc.	

A. Morris Capt RFA
for O Comdg 1/5 Yh RGA

Army Form C. 2118.

WAR DIARY
or
INTELLIGENCE SUMMARY
(Erase heading not required.)

"Confidential"

War --- Diary
of
2/8 Medium Trench Mortar Battery
From 1.2.19 to 28.2.19

Vol VI

Army Form C. 2118.

WAR DIARY
or
INTELLIGENCE SUMMARY.
(Erase heading not required.)

Instructions regarding War Diaries and Intelligence Summaries are contained in F. S. Regs., Part II. and the Staff Manual respectively. Title pages will be prepared in manuscript.

Place	Date	Hour	Summary of Events and Information	Remarks and references to Appendices
Sth Field.	28.2.17		Battery employed building Stevenson huts etc.	See
			C Morris Capt RFA	
			for O Comdg 47 Bde	

CONFIDENTIAL.

8th DIVISIONAL ARTILLERY.

WAR DIARY

OF

"W.X.Y.Z." Trench Mortar Batteries

From 1.3.17 To 31.3.17

(VOLUME VII)

With Appendices Nos. ....

Army Form C. 2118.

WAR DIARY
or
INTELLIGENCE SUMMARY.
(Erase heading not required.)

CONFIDENTIAL

WAR DIARY

OF

X/8 TRENCH MORTAR BATTERY

FROM. 1-3-17 To 31-3-17

Vol 2.

Army Form C. 2118.

WAR DIARY
or
INTELLIGENCE SUMMARY.
(Erase heading not required.)

Instructions regarding War Diaries and Intelligence Summaries are contained in F.S. Regs., Part II. and the Staff Manual respectively. Title pages will be prepared in manuscript.

Place	Date	Hour	Summary of Events and Information	Remarks and references to Appendices
Le- Forest	1-3-17 to		Building gun emplacements, carrying ammunition, constructing dug-out.	
	3-3-17		Two guns prepared for action.	
S.W. Corner	4-3-17		Two guns fired for 50 minutes during infantry attack. 58 rounds fired.	
St Pierre Vaast Wood.	5-3-17		Two guns fired during counter attack. 33 rounds fired.	
"	10-3-17		Gun detachments and guns kept in readiness for further counter attacks —	
"	11-3-17		Occasional registering rounds fired —	
"	12-3-17		Gun teams withdrawn to back area, two guns complete left in support line	
"	13-3-17 →			
"	14-3-17		Guns sent over again stand by to fire on enemy front line system. Working parties start to construct further two gun emplacements.	
"	15-3-17		Infantry occupy enemy front line system, fire orders cancelled gun crews withdrawn to back area.	
"	16-3-17		Fatigues. Road mending etc	
"	23-3-17 →			
"	24-3-17		Guns and Beds withdrawn from trenches to back area.	
	25-3-17		Haliques	

Army Form C. 2118.

WAR DIARY
or
INTELLIGENCE SUMMARY.
(Erase heading not required.)

Instructions regarding War Diaries and Intelligence Summaries are contained in F. S. Regs., Part II. and the Staff Manual respectively. Title pages will be prepared in manuscript.

Place	Date	Hour	Summary of Events and Information	Remarks and references to Appendices
Le Forest	26/3/17		General fatigues. Road mending. Repairing billets w/ Meisdains.	
	27/3/17			

R H Campbell Brown Lt.
o.C. У/87 M.B.T.

Army Form C. 2118.

WAR DIARY
or
INTELLIGENCE SUMMARY.
(Erase heading not required.)

SECRET

War Diary of
Y/8 Trench Mortar Battery

From 1.III.17 To 31.III.17

VOLUME II

Army Form C. 2118.

WAR DIARY
or
INTELLIGENCE SUMMARY.
(Erase heading not required.)

Instructions regarding War Diaries and Intelligence Summaries are contained in F.S. Regs., Part II. and the Staff Manual respectively. Title pages will be prepared in manuscript.

Place	Date	Hour	Summary of Events and Information	Remarks and references to Appendices
NEAR BOUCHAVESNES	4.III.17		Digging gun-pits and remaining in action for use if desired. C.E.	
	15.III.17		Fired 6 rounds at strong point in BREMEN TRENCH with good effect. C.E.	
	15.III.17		Withdrew from line. C.E.	
	16.III.17 to 31.III.17		Road-making and general fatigues. C.E.	

Allen Ellis a/Lieut. RFA
O.C. Y/15 T.M. Batt.

"SECRET"

War Diary of

Z/8 TRENCH MORTAR BATTERY.

From 1.VII.17 to 31.VII.17

VOLUME II

Army Form C. 2118.

WAR DIARY
or
INTELLIGENCE SUMMARY.
(Erase heading not required.)

Instructions regarding War Diaries and Intelligence Summaries are contained in F. S. Regs., Part II. and the Staff Manual respectively. Title pages will be prepared in manuscript.

Place	Date	Hour	Summary of Events and Information	Remarks and references to Appendices
Near LE FOREST.	From 1.10.17 to 31.10.19.		Road mending & general fatigues &c.	

A Mach RFA O/C for
O.C. Z/8 T.M.B.

Army Form C. 2118.

WAR DIARY
or
INTELLIGENCE SUMMARY.
(Erase heading not required.)

Place	Date	Hour	Summary of Events and Information	Remarks and references to Appendices
	13/2/17		Battery employed repairing roads leading Bapaume Army Rd	
			repaired River Ochel of Brooks	
			Attended Barrister	
			O'Connelly w/s Lut. T. Mr. Co	

Army Form C. 2118.

WAR DIARY
or
INTELLIGENCE SUMMARY.
(Erase heading not required.)

— Confidential —

War — Diary.

W/6 Heavy Trench Mortar Battery

From 1.3.1917 To 31.3.1917

Vol II

CONFIDENTIAL.

8th DIVISIONAL ARTILLERY.

WAR DIARY

OF

W. X. Y. Z. Trench Mortar Batteries

From 1.4.17. To 30.4.17.

(VOLUME VII)

With Appendices Nos. 1

Army Form C. 2118.

WAR DIARY
or
INTELLIGENCE SUMMARY.
(Erase heading not required.)

Place	Date	Hour	Summary of Events and Information	Remarks and references to Appendices
In the field	1-4-17 to 27-4-17		Battery employed on repair of roads, etc.	
	28-4-17 to 30-4-17		One gun in action on Dundee Road 200* S.E. of GONNELIEU CHURCH."	

O.M.
Capt R.G.A.
Comdg W/8 Ay T.M.B.

Army Form C. 2118.

WAR DIARY
or
INTELLIGENCE SUMMARY.
(Erase heading not required.)

Instructions regarding War Diaries and Intelligence Summaries are contained in F. S. Regs., Part II. and the Staff Manual respectively. Title pages will be prepared in manuscript.

Place	Date	Hour	Summary of Events and Information	Remarks and references to Appendices
HAUT-ALLAINES	1/4/17		Moved from LEFOREST to HAUT-ALLAINES	
"	2/4/17 to 20/4/17		Repairing billets in HAUT-ALLAINES. Road making and general fatigues	
	21/4/17 to 25/4/17		General fatigues for 8th Div. Art.y and Amm.n Column	
	26/4/17		Practice with German Light-Minenwerfen	
	30/4/17		Half Battery left HAUT-ALLAINES to go into action with captured German minen w. Other half battery fatigues	

A. S. Richardson?
M/Major O.C. 8 T.M.B.

Army Form C. 2118.

WAR DIARY
or
INTELLIGENCE SUMMARY.
(Erase heading not required.)

Instructions regarding War Diaries and Intelligence Summaries are contained in F. S. Regs., Part II. and the Staff Manual respectively. Title pages will be prepared in manuscript.

Place	Date	Hour	Summary of Events and Information	Remarks and references to Appendices
LE FOREST	1/4/17 6-29/4/17		Fatigues, salving ammunition, empty cartridge cases and R.E. Material	
	23/4/17		Marched from LE FOREST to HAUT-ALLAINES	
HAUT ALLAINES	24/4/17 to 30/4/17		General Fatigues at 8th Div. Arty.	

Orchestra
WRFA from Y/8 T.M.B.

Army Form C. 2118.

WAR DIARY
or
INTELLIGENCE SUMMARY

(Erase heading not required.)

Instructions regarding War Diaries and Intelligence Summaries are contained in F. S. Regs., Part II. and the Staff Manual respectively. Title Pages will be prepared in manuscript.

Place	Date	Hour	Summary of Events and Information	Remarks and references to Appendices
HARG - ALLAINES.	1 - 4 - 1917.		Ranks and ammunition fatigues for 2nd Divisionary Artillery.	
	25 - 4 - 1917			16.a.m.
VAUX - en - AMIENOIS.	26 - 4 - 1917 to 30 - 4 - 1917		Course of instruction at the Army School of Instruction VAUX - en - AMIENOIS.	12 a.m.

George Munro Lieut.
O.C. 2/8 T.M. Batt.

CONFIDENTIAL.

8th DIVISIONAL ARTILLERY.

WAR DIARY

OF

W. X. Y. Z. Trench Mortar Batteries

From 1.5.17 To 31.5.17.

(VOLUME VIII)

With Appendices Nos. ....

Army Form C. 2118.

WAR DIARY
or
INTELLIGENCE SUMMARY.
(Erase heading not required.)

Confidential

War ---- Diary
of
W/8 Heavy Trench Mortar Battery

From 1.5.16 To 31.5.16

Vol VIII

Army Form C. 2118.

WAR DIARY
or
INTELLIGENCE SUMMARY.
(Erase heading not required.)

Instructions regarding War Diaries and Intelligence Summaries are contained in F. S. Regs., Part II. and the Staff Manual respectively. Title pages will be prepared in manuscript.

Place	Date	Hour	Summary of Events and Information	Remarks and references to Appendices
NURLU	1-5-17 to 16-5-17		One heavy trench mortar & two captured German light Minenwerfer in action 200 yds S.E. of GONNELIEU. Three trench mortar shells exploded work in enemy strong points. Hostile mined at between 600 & 1000 yards range.	
	17. 5. 17		Moved to neighbourhood of DICKEBUSCHE.	
DICKEBUSCHE	24. 5. 17			
	25-5-17 to 31. 5. 17		Preparing Gun positions & digging dug outs at I.28.d.4.4 to I.3op.A.6.6. Belgium Map.	

A Munro Capt R.A.
O.C. No 1/6 Siy T.M.B

Army Form C. 2118.

WAR DIARY
or
INTELLIGENCE SUMMARY.
(Erase heading not required.)

CONFIDENTIAL

WAR DIARY

OF

X/8 Trench Mortar Battery

FROM 1-5-17 TO 31-5-17

VOL VIII

Sh Bths. LSA
to OC /s M-B

Army Form C. 2118.

WAR DIARY
or
INTELLIGENCE SUMMARY.
(Erase heading not required.)

Shorncliffe fn fsr

Instructions regarding War Diaries and Intelligence Summaries are contained in F. S. Regs., Part II. and the Staff Manual respectively. Title pages will be prepared in manuscript.

Place	Date	Hour	Summary of Events and Information	Remarks and references to Appendices
HAUT-ALLAINES	9/5/17 to 13/5/17		General fatigues, Assistant Drill and Kit Inspections	
HAUT-ALLAINES	14/5/17 to 19/5/17		Physical drill, re-drilling in accordance with DIVISION PROGRAMME	
	20/5/17		Marched from HAUT-ALLAINES to Camp 112	
CAMP 112	21/5/17		Paraded in camp and fatigues	
	22/5/17		Left Camp 112 and entrained at EDGEHILL SIDING	
ARQUES	23/5/17		Detrained at ARQUES	
	24/5/17		Proceeded by lorry to neighbourhood of DICKEBUSCH	
DICKEBUSCH	25/5/17 to 31/5/17		Preparing Mortar emplacements ready for action	

Army Form C. 2118.

WAR DIARY
or
INTELLIGENCE SUMMARY.
(Erase heading not required.)

WAR DIARY
OF
Y/8 TRENCH MORTAR BATTERY
FROM 1/5/17 TO 31/5/17.
VOL VIII

Army Form C. 2118.

WAR DIARY
or
INTELLIGENCE SUMMARY.
(Erase heading not required.)

Instructions regarding War Diaries and Intelligence Summaries are contained in F. S. Regs., Part II. and the Staff Manual respectively. Title pages will be prepared in manuscript.

Place	Date	Hour	Summary of Events and Information	Remarks and references to Appendices
HAUT-ALLAINES	1/5/17 to 15/5/17		General Fatigues, Gas Helmet-drill, and Kit Inspections	
-do-	16/5/17 to 19/5/17		Physical drill & re-drilling in accordance with Divisional Programme	
	20/5/17		Marched from HAUT ALLAINES to CAMP 112	
CAMP 112	21/5/17 22/5/17		Parades in Camp - fatigues	
			Left CAMP 112 and entrained at EDGE HILL SIDING	
ARQUES	23/5/17 24/5/17		detrained at ARQUES.	
			Proceeded by lorry to neighbourhood of DICKEBUSH	
DICKEBUSH	25/5/17 to 31/5/17		Preparing positions in the line ready for action	

(Signed) Richard
Lt-Col OC 1/5 T.M.B

Army Form C. 2118.

WAR DIARY
or
INTELLIGENCE SUMMARY
(Erase heading not required.)

Confidential.

WAR DIARY
of
2/8 T.M. Batt.
from 1-5-17 to 31-5-17
(Volume VIII)

Army Form C. 2118.

WAR DIARY
or
INTELLIGENCE SUMMARY
(Erase heading not required.)

Instructions regarding War Diaries and Intelligence Summaries are contained in F. S. Regs., Part II. and the Staff Manual respectively. Title Pages will be prepared in manuscript.

Place	Date	Hour	Summary of Events and Information	Remarks and references to Appendices
VAUX-en-AMIÉNOIS.	1-5-17 to 7-5-17		Gunnery Instruction at Fourth Army T.M. School. Vaux-en-Amiénois.	7.0M + 11.20H
NURLU.	8-5-17 to 14-5-17		Fatigues (move ammo dump) for Divisionnal Artillery.	7.0M
HAUT-ALLAINES	15-5-17 to 19-5-17		Intensive training.	7.0M
	20-5-17 to 24-5-17		Line & trench.	7.0M
SPOIL BANK SECTOR (YPRES SALIENT)	25-5-17 to 31-5-17		Reinforced 2/4? T.M. Battery. Repairs and improvement to dugouts.	4.0M

Geo.O.Munro, Lieut.
O.C. 2/6 7M. Batt.

2449 Wt. W14957/M90 750,000 1/16 J.B.C. & A. Forms/C.2118/12.

CONFIDENTIAL.

8th DIVISIONAL ARTILLERY.

WAR DIARY

OF

W.X.Y.Z. T.M. Batteries

From 1st June To 30 June 1917.

(VOLUME X)

With Appendices Nos. —

Army Form C. 2118.

WAR DIARY
or
INTELLIGENCE SUMMARY.
(Erase heading not required.)

CONFIDENTIAL.

WAR DIARY.

of

M/8 T.M. Batt.

from 1-6-17 to 30-6-17.

(Volume X)

with appendix.

Army Form C. 2118.

WAR DIARY
or
INTELLIGENCE SUMMARY.
(Erase heading not required.)

Instructions regarding War Diaries and Intelligence Summaries are contained in F. S. Regs., Part II. and the Staff Manual respectively. Title pages will be prepared in manuscript.

Place	Date	Hour	Summary of Events and Information	Remarks and references to Appendices
Ypres Salient	1.6.17 to 7.6.17		Battery in action in Ravine I.34.a. firing 350 rounds on enemy redoubt and strong points. Relieved with Good effect. Enemy shelled two lines, before infantry came at ammunition dump before relieved. Battery withdrawn from line at 3 a.m. on 7/6 accommodated back to Rest Area in OUDERDOM. Capt. G.H. MORRIS R.G.A. (later wounded on 2.6.17)	
	8.6.17 to 11.6.17		Rest billets in OUDERDOM. nothing to record.	
CAISTRE	11.6.17 to 14.6.17		Moved by motor lorries to CAISTRE on 11th. Nothing to record	
Ypres Salient	14.6.17		Battery marched back to L.14.13.c (Belgian Sheet 28 N.W.) to begin work again in the salient in either future until of use action however	

Signature
Capt
for O.C. W/8 S.M. B

Army Form C. 2118.

WAR DIARY
or
INTELLIGENCE SUMMARY.
(Erase heading not required.)

Instructions regarding War Diaries and Intelligence Summaries are contained in F. S. Regs., Part II. and the Staff Manual respectively. Title pages will be prepared in manuscript.

Place	Date	Hour	Summary of Events and Information	Remarks and references to Appendices
YPRES SALIENT.	16-6-17.		Digging positions for Heavy Trench Mortar carried out. Two positions in front of BEEK TRENCH (at I.11.a.8.9) dug. One off WEST LANE about was attempted on the shell line also 105 heavy to continue work. (I.11.c.6.6.) Scheme cancelled now non-(cannot owing to the continuous shelling on WEST LANE, which even the enemy communication trench from this area.	P.C.M. Guerrima. Kent OC. 4/8 7th Batt.
	30-6-17.			

Army Form C. 2118.

WAR DIARY
or
INTELLIGENCE SUMMARY.
(Erase heading not required.)

CONFIDENTIAL

WAR DIARY

X/8 Trench Mortar Battery

From 1-6-17 To 30-6-17

Vol IX

G.P.Osburn Lieut
Initials
30-6-17 OC X/8 T M B^{ty}

Army Form C. 2118.

WAR DIARY
INTELLIGENCE SUMMARY.
(Erase heading not required.)

Place	Date	Hour	Summary of Events and Information	Remarks and references to Appendices
Hill 60	1/6/17		The battery was in action in the Ravine wood on the rgt of Hill 60. Three of the guns had their fire directed on the enemy's wire and front line, while the fourth was laid on the support line in case of an S.O.S. The battery was supporting X/47 Battery.	
	7/6/17		Personnel withdrawn from the line	
Dickebush	7/6/17	8-10	General fatigues in camp	
	9/6/17			
Caestre	10/6/17		Guns withdrawn from the line. Proceeded by lorries to Caestre. Fatigues in camp; inspection of kit and guns etc. Marched from Caestre to Oudezeem.	
	15/6/17 to 16/6/17			
Oudezeem	16/6/17 to 30/6/17		The battery carrying ammunition to positions in the line by Ravelsberg Wood belonging to Z and Y Batteries	

In the field
30-6-17 O.C. X/8 T.M. Bty
G.R.Rhoun Lieut

Army Form C. 2118.

WAR DIARY
or
INTELLIGENCE SUMMARY.
(Erase heading not required.)

CONFIDENTIAL

WAR DIARY

Y/8 TRENCH MORTAR BATTERY

From 1.6.17 to 30.6.17

Volume IX

Army Form C. 2118.

WAR DIARY
or
INTELLIGENCE SUMMARY.
(Erase heading not required.)

Instructions regarding War Diaries and Intelligence Summaries are contained in F. S. Regs., Part II. and the Staff Manual respectively. Title pages will be prepared in manuscript.

Place	Date	Hour	Summary of Events and Information	Remarks and references to Appendices
Ypres Salient	1/6/17 to 7/6/17	—	Battery in action in Reserve Wood S.E. of Ypres firing nightly 400 rounds ammunition from Hun. Battery withdrawn from line on morning of 7th & sent home to refit & recuperate.	
OUDERDOM	8/6/17 to 31/6/17		Rest billets near OUDERDOM. Refitting to normal.	
CAESTRE	1/6/17 to 15/6/17		Moved by route march on 11th to CAESTRE & remained until the 15th. Battery & vehicles to road.	
	15/6/17 to 30/6/17		Moved back to an OUDERDOM - Westoutre embankment north of RAILWAY WOOD near YPRES concealed and commenced in Tile 30th. Lieut. A.S. RICHARDS R.F.A. killed in action on 25.6.17.	

Lieut Allan Capt.

for O.C. Y/8 T.M.B.

Army Form C. 2118.

WAR DIARY
or
INTELLIGENCE SUMMARY.
(Erase heading not required.)

CONFIDENTIAL

WAR DIARY
of
2/8 TRENCH MORTAR BATTERY.
From 1-6-17 to 30-7-17.

Volume IV

Army Form C. 2118.

WAR DIARY
or
INTELLIGENCE SUMMARY.
(Erase heading not required.)

Place	Date	Hour	Summary of Events and Information	Remarks and references to Appendices
YPRES SALIENT	1-6-17 to 7-6-17		The battery, as reinforcement to X/47 T.M. Batt. carried out firing on enemy's wire and defences in front and support lines from O.7.a.6.50.65. O.3.d.55.90. (OAK TRENCH, OAK SUPPORT, OAK AVENUE & OAK ALLEY.) The wire was effectively cut, and trenches fairly well damaged (as was proved by examination subsequent to the attack on 7/6/17. Best observation was to be found in the front line at about O.3.b.50.40. but from this one only front line trench could be seen after about 15 the ground front wire was examined from about T.33.d.60.10. (KING ST TUNNEL O.P.) During the six days' bombardment the Mortar programme allowed for firing 50 rounds per day but the supply of ammunition and behaviour of carrying parties which were both highly unsatisfactory and unreliable did not allow of even this small amount being fired. Average ammunition expenditure was 60 rounds per day. One foreman gunner wounded on 4/6/17 resulting in the only casualty in the bombardment - 1 NCO killed. Three pits were handed over by 49th Division, each an also previously to some were marked feature on the map, and showing distinctly on aero-photographs. A fourth was built and carefully camouflaged - this pit was even most in the bombardment	

Army Form C. 2118.

WAR DIARY
or
INTELLIGENCE SUMMARY.
(Erase heading not required.)

Instructions regarding War Diaries and Intelligence Summaries are contained in F. S. Regs., Part II. and the Staff Manual respectively. Title pages will be prepared in manuscript.

Place	Date	Hour	Summary of Events and Information	Remarks and references to Appendices
YPRES	1-6-17		Firing was discontinued on 6-6-17.	
SALIENT	6			
	7-6-17		On 7-6-17 party of 15 (with 10 of X/147 Batt.) proceeded with bombs from dumps in NORFOLK LANE (about O.4.a.10.63.) 6 Broken Ridge at O.4.8.2.4. (following in rear of the infantry assault) two journeys were made. One man was killed and four wounded.	G.O.M.
			The battery withdrawn from action.	
	8-6-17 to 10-6-17		Battery in rest billets between OUDEZDOM and DICKEBUSCH (H.26.C.2.8. sheet 28.NW.) (Belgium sheet 28.NW)	G.O.M.
	11-6-17			
CAESTRE	11-6-17		Rest in camp near CAESTRE	G.O.M.
WINNIPEG CAMP	14-6-17		Rest billets at H.13.C. (Belgium Sheet 28 NW) (WINNIPEG CAMP)	G.O.M.
NORTH of YPRES	16-6-17		The battery took over positions from 2/55 T.M.B. these positions were found to be in a very bad state. Work was started immediately to improve and make new positions.	
			Two gun positions are completed at Sunken Rd trench off West Lane at 7:11:b:50:20. and were registered on enemys trench and wire between 7:12:a:00:55. and 7:12.a.30:30. on the 19-6-17.	
			A large bomb store has been completed of Sunken Rd trench holding 150 bombs.	
			Two gun positions off Crater trench 7:11.b:65:25 are nearly completed, and two gun positions at 7:11:80:65 are being constructed	

Army Form C. 2118.

WAR DIARY
or
INTELLIGENCE SUMMARY
(Erase heading not required.)

Instructions regarding War Diaries and Intelligence Summaries are contained in F. S. Regs., Part II. and the Staff Manual respectively. Title Pages will be prepared in manuscript.

Place	Date	Hour	Summary of Events and Information	Remarks and references to Appendices
	25-6-17		The battery received a request from the O.C. of the battalion in the line to assist in a raid that was to take place that night. We registered on enemy's trench + wire from 7.12.a 30.10 to 7.12.a 25.35 during the day. The night of the raid we were allowed 8 minutes to get off as many rounds as possible from the two guns in action. We were able to get off 21 rounds before the signal to cease fire was received. Next day we were thanked by the O.C. of the battalion in the line for our part in the raid, which resulted in the capture of a prisoner. The battery has received orders to fire very little, 10 rounds is about the amount fired per day. Work is done chiefly at night to avoid enemy's balloon + aeroplane observation.	

30/6/17
J.J. Mc Ash Lieut
O.C. Z/8 T.M.B.

CONFIDENTIAL.

8th DIVISIONAL ARTILLERY.

WAR DIARY

OF

W. X. Y. + Z. T.M. Batteries

From 1st July To 30 July 1917

(VOLUME X)

With APPENDICES Nos.

Army Form C. 2118.

WAR DIARY
or
INTELLIGENCE SUMMARY.
(Erase heading not required.)

Confidential

War Diary
of
W/8 Trench Mortar Battery
From 1-7-1917 to 30-7-1917

Vol II.

Army Form C. 2118.

WAR DIARY
or
INTELLIGENCE SUMMARY.
(Erase heading not required.)

Instructions regarding War Diaries and Intelligence Summaries are contained in F. S. Regs., Part II. and the Staff Manual respectively. Title pages will be prepared in manuscript.

Place	Date	Hour	Summary of Events and Information	Remarks and references to Appendices
East of Ypres	1.7.17		Work proceeded on three positions. One of these handed over to Australian T.M.B. The others abandoned thro' being destroyed by shell fire. Another position was then selected and an O.P. chosen that commanded a view of the entire field of fire. Work proceed on two gun positions until they were completed on	
	20.7.17		the 20-7-17 and the guns installed. One gun never was in action owing to its structural faults. The targets given us were situated in Chateau Wood. We were also to fire to the west of Bellewaarde Lake.	
	21.7.17		Ten rounds were fired on above zones. Enemy aircraft hindered firing to large extent.	
	22.7.17		Sixteen rounds fired. The error of gun fairly large both width and length. This made firing to west of lake very difficult. 25 rounds fired. The gun developed heat rapidly, particularly when rate of firing was over 5 in the hour. The targets in Chateau	

Army Form C. 2118.

WAR DIARY
or
INTELLIGENCE SUMMARY.
(Erase heading not required.)

Instructions regarding War Diaries and Intelligence Summaries are contained in F. S. Regs., Part II. and the Staff Manual respectively. Title pages will be prepared in manuscript.

Place	Date	Hour	Summary of Events and Information	Remarks and references to Appendices
	23.7.17		Wood were effectively engaged.	
	24.7.17		Thirty rounds fired on same targets. Firing interrupted both by enemy shelling and aeroplane activity	
	25.7.17		Thirty four rounds fired at same targets and others in same zone. Observation was good and many effective bursts were observed. Rain interrupted firing. One round requiring as many as four fuzes. When weather cleared enemy shelled all round position. 13 rounds were fired	
	26.7.17		Gun pit giving way. Platform for gun strengthened. Thirteen rounds fired considerable precaution noted	
	27.7.17		39 rounds fired. Twenty of these at a zone just beyond chateau wood. Many fell in zone. Sandbags and timber were observed in air after several bursts	
	28.7.17		43 rounds fired at targets given us. The best needs rebuilding. Fire was effective	
	29.7.17		Personnel withdrawn from trenches & rds. fired.	

Army Form C. 2118.

WAR DIARY
or
INTELLIGENCE SUMMARY
(Erase heading not required.)

Place	Date	Hour	Summary of Events and Information	Remarks and references to Appendices
Summary			During construction of gun positions work was carried on almost entirely by night. The first position chosen was abandoned by enemy fire and absorbed by us before firing a shot. The second position proved admirable. It received several direct hits but remained concealed from enemy until personnel was withdrawn. The work of preparing gun positions and bringing up ammunition at night was very arduous and during this period the battery suffered the following casualties; on the 5th Gr. Wallace wounded on 14th Dr. Ahern I.C. wounded in action, on 16th Sgt. Glendening killed in action, on the 18th 2/Lt. Milligan gassed and sent to hospital. The guns proved a T.M. (Russian gun) while having a splendid range possessed a very large 50% 3 in. tooth length and breadth. Individual targets could not be taken on. Duds were very few. Firing in wet weather was unsatisfactory owing to stalk of fuzes.	

H.R. Latimer 2/Lt HAC
W/O TM13

Army Form C. 2118.

WAR DIARY
or
INTELLIGENCE SUMMARY.
(Erase heading not required.)

CONFIDENTIAL

WAR DIARY

X/8 Trench Mortar Battery

From 1-7-16 To 31-7-17

Vol II

Army Form C. 2118.

WAR DIARY
or
INTELLIGENCE SUMMARY.
(Erase heading not required.)

Instructions regarding War Diaries and Intelligence
Summaries are contained in F. S. Regs., Part II.
and the Staff Manual respectively. Title pages
will be prepared in manuscript.

Place	Date	Hour	Summary of Events and Information	Remarks and references to Appendices
	July 1st		Battery carrying ammunition to Mortar positions on the line by railway Wood belonging to Y-Z 13 g	
	1st & 5th		One Officer and 5 other Ranks attended a course of 6" Newton Mortar at 2nd Army School	
	2/7/17		Battery take over 6 inch Newton Mortars. Clear up guns and general fatigues in camp	
	3/7/17		Battery carrying ammunition to Mortar positions in the line by railway Wood belonging to Y-Z 13 g	
	4/7/17		General fatigues in camp. One N.C.O. + 4 Gunner attended a Course of 1" N.M. at 2nd Army School	
	5/7/17		Battery carrying ammunition to Mortar positions in the line by railway Wood belonging to Y-Z 13 g	
	6/7/17		Battery Gun Drill with 6" Newton Mortars and General fatigues in camp	
	7/7/17		Battery carrying ammunition to Mortar positions in the line by railway Wood belonging to Y-Z 13 g	
	8/7/17		Battery Gun Drill and General fatigues	
	9th & 15th 7/17		Battery in the line making emplacements for the new 6" Newton Mortars	
	16/7/17		3 Gunners attend a course of 6" Newton Mortars at 2nd Army School	
	17/7/17		First 6 inch Newton Mortar in action N° I Gun in action at J 11 d 5950 Zero line on true bearing of 119°	
	18.7.17		N° 2 Gun in action at J 11 A 5.5. 55 Zero Line on true bearing of 120°.	
	19/7/17 to 22/7/19		The following target were engaged 214 rounds being fired. Ignorance Trench from J 18 b 2040 to J 18 b 7010	
	23/7/19		20 Rounds were fired on the following target Ignorance Trench from J 18 b 2050 to J 18 b 5010	

2353 Wt. W2544/1454 700,000 5/15 D.D.&L. A.D.S.S./Forms/C. 2118.

WAR DIARY
or
INTELLIGENCE SUMMARY.
(Erase heading not required.)

Army Form C. 2118.

Instructions regarding War Diaries and Intelligence Summaries are contained in F. S. Regs., Part II. and the Staff Manual respectively. Title pages will be prepared in manuscript.

Place	Date	Hour	Summary of Events and Information	Remarks and references to Appendices
	24/7/17		No 2 Gun and position were completely Destroyed by enemy shell fire.	
	25/7/17		20 rounds were fired from No 1 Gun on Ignorance Trench and Ignorance Support on the latter target on of our shells exploded on enemy small ammunition dump.	
	26/7/17		25 rounds were fired on Ignorance Support and Ignorance Reserve.	
	27/7/17		50 Rounds were fired on Target a.z. J12 d 65.20	
	28/7/17		One officer and five other ranks remain in the line. Remainder being withdrawn	
	"		50 Rounds fired at Hooge Crater and vicinity	
	29/7/17		60 rounds fired at J 18 b 05-85 to J1.2. B.1. Personnel withdrawn from the line to the back area. Total number of round fired from July 17 - 29 = 4440	
	30/7/17		General Fatigues in Camp	
	31-7-7		DITTO	

C. W. Hardyman 2/Lt
X/27. M.B.

Army Form C. 2118.

WAR DIARY
or
INTELLIGENCE SUMMARY.
(Erase heading not required.)

War Diary
of
Y/8 Trench Mortar Battery
From
1/7/1917 to 31/7/1917
Vol III

WAR DIARY
or
INTELLIGENCE SUMMARY.
(Erase heading not required.)

Army Form C. 2118.

Place	Date	Hour	Summary of Events and Information	Remarks and references to Appendices
BUSSEBOOM	1/7/17 to 2/7/17		Work proceeded with on protective snow fences also to 25th Div. and more snow fences also to no. 5, Z Battery	
	10/7/17 to 15/7/17		Snow so as daily at enemy wire also the wire being cleared and cut by the 15th inst. During this period satisfaction in the work being expressed in letters by the Corps & Div. Commander in the trenches an operation in full swing such as being freely an experience that this was an extreme German counter attack on the 16th was soon called off by them. We are almost begging enemy to launch an attack. The wire itself was broken from end to end. The night of 17th Given to reports that hostile troops were massed behind our trenches.	
	18/7/17 to 21/7/17		Snow so as pen day at the 15th view of experience at the evening English/Eng works. At hour frost/4 p.m. defendable of Marin that's during went to Prov day & hero infantry into franca, but he could see damage truck in aim keep	

Instructions regarding War Diaries and Intelligence Summaries are contained in F. S. Regs., Part II. and the Staff Manual respectively. Title pages will be prepared in manuscript.

WAR DIARY
or
INTELLIGENCE SUMMARY.
(Erase heading not required.)

Army Form C. 2118.

Place	Date	Hour	Summary of Events and Information	Remarks and references to Appendices
BOSSEBOOM			of knocking up trench boards &c. This was done fairly frequently and one day 2 men were ordered to [illegible] down from the tunnel into the lake	
	20/7/17 to 25/7/17		We continued to fire 80 to 100 rds per day, on the night 21/22 we were very badly gassed and the tunnels shelled with armour piercing shells of a large calibre.	
			On the 22nd at the request of the MO of the Battn in the line, our men were used as stretcher bearers to the casualties gassed and hurt in the collapse of the tunnel. During the period 18/25 Enemy's artillery was abnormally active the whole time.	
	25/7/17 to 29/7/17		Received orders to fire only if enemy attempted to repair his wire or any strong point at the request of the Battn Commander in the line. This request was never asked for.	
	29/7/17		Withdrew from the line	

[illegible signature]

Army Form C. 2118.

WAR DIARY
or
INTELLIGENCE SUMMARY
(Erase heading not required.)

Confidential

WAR DIARY
of
X/8 Trench Mortar Battery.

From 1-7-1917 to 30-7-1917.

VOL II

WAR DIARY
or
INTELLIGENCE SUMMARY
(Erase heading not required.)

Army Form C. 2118.

Place	Date	Hour	Summary of Events and Information	Remarks and references to Appendices
NORTH OF YPRES	1/7/17 to 11/7/17		Work proceeded on gun positions at 1.11.b.75.15 off West Lane and were completed by the 7th, the making of gun positions completed and in action.	
	12/7/17 to 15/7/17		Two extra gun positions completed in Crater Trench which were taken over by Y Battery on the 12th inst. From the 1st to the 7th we had orders to fire 25 rds per day at wire 1.11.b.100.90 to 1.12.a 30.30 (Idea Trench) from the 8th to the 13th 50 rds per day were fired. From the 14th 150 to 200 rds per day were fired at wire and Idea trench from 1.11.b.100.90 to 1.12.a 30.30. By the 19th all wire was cleared to the full extent of our zone and the front trench badly smashed to the satisfaction of the OC of battalion holding the sector.	
	15/7/17 to 19/7/17			
	20/7/17 to 25/7/17		On the 20th we fired on Idea Support. Observation was impossible from our OPs, so relied on map range excepting the extreme left (Idea Trench). During the night of the 21st we were heavily bombarded with gas shells. In the morning (22) we were again bombarded, the enemy using heavy armour piercing shells which penetrated tunnels at Railway Wood in which we were billeted during which period 1 NCO & 2 GUNNERS were gassed and sent to hospital. During the	

Army Form C. 2118.

WAR DIARY
or
INTELLIGENCE SUMMARY

(Erase heading not required.)

Instructions regarding War Diaries and Intelligence Summaries are contained in F.S. Regs., Part II. and the Staff Manual respectively. Title Pages will be prepared in manuscript.

Place	Date	Hour	Summary of Events and Information	Remarks and references to Appendices
	24/7/17 to 29/7/17	cont	afternoon at request of M.O. all available men of the battery acted as stretcher bearers carrying gassed and wounded men to MENIN RD aid post. There being over forty stretcher cases.	
	25/7/17		On the 25th received orders to fire only if enemy attempted to replace wire on his front line system or any strong point located by the infantry.	
	29/7/17			
	Summary		During the construction of gun positions work was chiefly carried out at night, on account of enemy's kite balloons overlooking the positions. When the positions were completed they proved to be strong and well concealed from enemy's fire. During the month No 1 Gun (off West Lane) and No 3 (Sunken Rd Trench) received direct hits doing a great amount of damage. The trenches leading to gun positions were badly knocked about on several occasions. The majority of our shooting was done under cover of our heavy artillery. During the firing we received very little retaliation but were frequently shelled by 77mm + 4.2s. It appeared that the enemy tried to locate our positions while we	

2449 Wt. W14957/M90 750,000 1/16 J.B.C. & A. Forms/C.2118/12.

WAR DIARY
or
INTELLIGENCE SUMMARY
(Erase heading not required.)

Army Form C. 2118.

Place	Date	Hour	Summary of Events and Information	Remarks and references to Appendices
Summary cont			& afterwards retaliated were firing. From the 1st to the 15th we were troubled a considerable amount by the enemy firing aerial darts during the evenings & nights. After the 15th this became less frequent and towards the end of month ceased altogether. West Lane leading to Railway Wood was heavily bombarded day & night, causing a great amount of difficulty to those proceeding to & from the trenches. The portion of the trench which came in for the hottest of the enemy's fire was that part 200 yds either side of the railway. The quietest time as a rule to proceed along West Lane was 1 hour after dawn. Railway Wood & vicinity were shelled at intervals daily, during the month, towards the latter end the trenches were in a very bad state. On the 29th inst all personnel were withdrawn from the line leaving the guns in action.	

J. Hubbuck Lg R.F.A.
O.C. Z/8. T.M.B.

CONFIDENTIAL.

8th DIVISIONAL ARTILLERY.

WAR DIARY
OF
W. X. Y. Z. T.M. Batteries

From 31.7. To 31.8.17

(VOLUME II)

With Appendices Nos.

Army Form C. 2118.

WAR DIARY
or
INTELLIGENCE SUMMARY.

(Erase heading not required.)

Place	Date	Hour	Summary of Events and Information	Remarks and references to Appendices
Cauderlon	1.8.17 2/3/4/5/17		Battery on general fatigues etc in camp.	
"	5.8.17		The Battery attended a ceremonial service for the late Capt. Walker (M.C.) killed in action near Ypres on the 18/7/17.	
"	6.8.17		No. 82452 Bomb. Perfect W.R. R.F.A. and No. 16906 Gunr. Barrett W. R.F.A. to J.M.B. were presented with the Military Medal, for gallantry and devotion to duty near Hill 60. on the 7/6/17, by the Corps Commander.	
"	7.8.17		Battery on General Fatigues etc in camp	
"	8.8.17		" " " " "	
"	9.8.17		Battery withdraw all guns from the line	
"	10.8.17		" Cleaning guns clothes etc	
"	11.8.17		" " " " "	
"	12.8.17		Attend morning Church Service	
"	13.8.17		Road making	
"	14.8.17		" " for Artillery	
"	15.8.17		" " " "	
"	16.8.17		General fatigues in camp.	

Army Form C. 2118.

WAR DIARY
or
INTELLIGENCE SUMMARY.
(Erase heading not required.)

Instructions regarding War Diaries and Intelligence Summaries are contained in F. S. Regs., Part II. and the Staff Manual respectively. Title pages will be prepared in manuscript.

Place	Date	Hour	Summary of Events and Information	Remarks and references to Appendices
Oudezeele	August 17/18		The Battery on general fatigues in camp.	
	19/8/17		The Battery employed in bringing damaged field guns out of action	
	20.8.17		" " " " " " "	
	21.8.17		" " " " " " "	
	22.8.17		" " " " " " "	
	23.8.17		" " " " " " "	
	24.8.17		" " " " " " "	
	25.8.17		" " " " " " "	
	26.8.17		" " " " " " "	
	27.8.17		" " " " " " "	
	28.8.17		Cleaning guns & overhauling stores	
	29.8.17		Battery moved from Oudezeele to Godeswaersvelde.	
Godeswaersveld	30/8/17		Camp fatigues &c &c	
	31/8/17		" " " "	

C. M. Harkins
Lieut. R.F.A.
O.C. 78. T.M. Batty

WAR DIARY
or
INTELLIGENCE SUMMARY.

Army Form C. 2118.

Place	Date	Hour	Summary of Events and Information	Remarks and references to Appendices
BUSSE BOOM	1/8/17 to 4/8/17		Withdrew guns from the line	
	6/8/17		Inspection by the Corps Commander, No 81325 Br Garwood R.H. presented with the M.M.	
	7/8/17		Inspection by the Divisional	
	8/8/17 to 13/8/17		Parades. Etc.	
	14/8/17 to 19/8/17		Working under R.E's. Road making in the forward area.	
	29/8/17 to 27/8/17		Salving Field Gun's etc	
	29/8/17		Moved by Motor Lorries to GODEWAERSVELDT.	
GODEWAERSVELDT.	30/8/17 to 31/8/17		Parades, Fatigues. Etc.	

A.J. Mackrient R.A.
OC 2/8 T.M. Bty.

Army Form C. 2118.

WAR DIARY
or
INTELLIGENCE SUMMARY.
(Erase heading not required.)

Instructions regarding War Diaries and Intelligence Summaries are contained in F.S. Regs., Part II. and the Staff Manual respectively. Title pages will be prepared in manuscript.

Place	Date	Hour	Summary of Events and Information	Remarks and references to Appendices
BUSSE-BOOM	1/7/17		Withdrew Guns from the Line	
	2/4/17 to 5/7/17		FATIGUES	
	6/7/17		Inspection by Corps Commander & presentation of medals (Nº 2452 P.T. Shufflebotham R.F.A. Y/12 T.M.Bty - M.M.) Inspection by Divisional Commander	
	7/7/17 8/7/17 to 9/7/17		Parades & Eli:	
	10/7/17 to 19/7/17		Working under R.E.s	
	20/7/17 to 27/7/17		Salving Guns & Eli: Jabber talk	
	28/7/17		Moved by motor lorry to GODEWAERSVELDT.	
	29/7/17 30/7/17		Parades & Eli:	
GODE=WAERSVELD	31/7/17			

A. Stewart Jr. R.A.
O.C. 1/6 T.9 B.

A. Stewart
O.C.
1/6 T.9 B.

Army Form C. 2118.

WAR DIARY
or
INTELLIGENCE SUMMARY.

(Erase heading not required.)

90/6 Heavy Trench Mortar B'y R.F.A.

Place	Date	Hour	Summary of Events and Information	Remarks and references to Appendices
YPRES	1-4/8/17		Withdrew mortars from the line	
	2-5/8/17		General fatigues	
	6.8.17		Inspection by Corps Commander & presentation of medals	
	7.8.17		Inspection by Divisional Commander	
	8.8.17 to 19.8.17		Parades & fatigues	
	20.8.17 to 27.8.17		Saving field guns	
	29.8.17		Moved by motor lorry to GODEWAERSVELDT	
	30.8.17 to 31.8.17		Parades etc	

G.P.Brown Capt. R.F.A.
O/c W/87.M.B'y

Army Form C. 2118.

WAR DIARY
or
INTELLIGENCE SUMMARY.
(Erase heading not required.)

Vol 16

Confidential
War - Diary
X/8 Trench Mortar Battery
From 1/9/17 to 30/9/17
Vol II

C. Hawkins Lieut
O.C. X/8 T.M. Bty

Army Form C. 2118.

WAR DIARY
or
INTELLIGENCE SUMMARY.
(Erase heading not required.)

Instructions regarding War Diaries and Intelligence Summaries are contained in F. S. Regs., Part II. and the Staff Manual respectively. Title pages will be prepared in manuscript.

Place	Date	Hour	Summary of Events and Information	Remarks and references to Appendices
Godewaersvelde	1-9-17		Moved from Godewaersvelde to Balleui	
Balleui	2-9-17		Fatigues in billets squaring up gun stores	
"	3-9-17		Fatigues in billets etc	
"	4-9-17		Battey parade for baths	
"	5-9-17		Cleaning guns + stores etc	
"	6-9-17		Battery move to new area. NEUVE EGLESE	
"			Gun cleaning etc	
Neuve Eglise	7-9-17			
"	8-9-17		Battery move from Neuve Eglise to Niepe in Motor Lorries	
"	9-9-17		Billet fatigues etc	
Niepe	10-9-17, 14-9-17		Parades etc	
	15-9-17		One Officer and 6 other Ranks proceed to the line and proceed to "Newton Mortar in placement No 82452 13" Perfect WR RFA proceeded to United Kingdom on 10 days Leave.	
	16-9-17		Two men proceed to the line with Rations remainder fatigues	
	17-9-17		Battery Parade for baths. No 36282 Corpl Smithson F. W. RFA proceeded to United Kingdom on 10 days leave.	
	18-9-17		Battery takes over two 6" Newton Mortars. Clean of Guns etc	

2353 Wt. W2544/1454 700,000 5/15 D. D. & L. A.D.S.S./Forms/C. 2118.

Army Form C. 2118.

WAR DIARY
or
INTELLIGENCE SUMMARY.
(Erase heading not required.)

Instructions regarding War Diaries and Intelligence Summaries are contained in F. S. Regs., Part II. and the Staff Manual respectively. Title pages will be prepared in manuscript.

Place	Date	Hour	Summary of Events and Information	Remarks and references to Appendices
NIEPPE	20/9/17		Two men proceed to line with rations. ML L mortar taken up to the line by G.S. Wagon and put into action N°1 Gun. Map ref C.42.10.85	
	21/9/17		Two men proceed to line with rations. Two others to Ordnance to draw Number of Spare parts	
	22/9/17		Fbg party of 1 N.C.O and 5 men proceed to the line. Remainder in billet-fatigues etc	
	23/9/17		One Officer and on N.C.O proceed to the line, Map Ref U.110. 55.10 to plan out a position for 6" Newton Mortar. Two men proceed to the line with rations, Remainder in billet. Church Service N°94777 2nd/Bundle H.J. R.F.A. and N°1936 Gnr Workhorn, R.F.A. proceeded to United Kingdom on 10 days leave	
	24/9/17		One Officer and 6 other Ranks proceed to the line to prepare L mortar emplacement. Map Ref U.110. 55.10	
	25/9/17		Fatigue Party of 6 men proceed to the line Map Ref C.42. 10.85	
	26/9/17		Two men proceed to the line with rations, remainder in billet baths	
	27/9/17		12 Rounds fired from N°1 Gun on Laundry & Laundry Wood. Map ref C.5c	
	28/9/17		10 " " " " " " " " " "	
	29/9/17		N°2 emplacement ready. Map ref C.42. 15.55	
	29/9/17		10 Rounds fired from N°L Gun on Laundry & Laundry Wood M.R. C. 5c	
	30/9/17		10 Rounds fired from N°L Gun on Laundry & Laundry Wood M.R. C.5c. Second Gun taken U.11.R. 55.10	

G.S. W. & Co A.D.S.S./Forth/C.2118.

Army Form C. 2118.

WAR DIARY
or
INTELLIGENCE SUMMARY.
(Erase heading not required.)

WAR DIARY
OF
V/8 TRENCH MORTAR BATTERY

FROM 1/9/17 TO 30/9/17

VOL II

Army Form C. 2118.

WAR DIARY
or
INTELLIGENCE SUMMARY.
(Erase heading not required.)

Instructions regarding War Diaries and Intelligence Summaries are contained in F. S. Regs., Part II. and the Staff Manual respectively. Title pages will be prepared in manuscript.

Place	Date	Hour	Summary of Events and Information	Remarks and references to Appendices
Godewaersvelde	1/9/17		Moved by lorry to Bailleul	
Bailleul	2/9/17 to 5/9/17		Parades & Bli.	
	6/9/17		Moved by lorry to Neuve Eglise	
Neuve Eglise	6/9/17 to 7/9/17		Moved to Nieppe	
Nieppe	8/9/17 to 18/9/17		Parades. Fatigues.	
	19/9/17 to 27/9/17		Working under R.E.s (O.P. constructing) (assisting) X/17 T.M.By. making gun position in the line.	
	28/9/17 to 30/9/17		Position selected in the line for B14.	
			B14 in the line making gun position.	

M. Stewart Lr. R.A.?
O.C. 46 T.O.B.

Army Form C. 2118.

WAR DIARY
or
INTELLIGENCE SUMMARY.
(Erase heading not required.)

CONFIDENTIAL

WAR DIARY

OF

Z/8 TRENCH MORTAR BATTERY.

From 1/9/17 to 30/9/17.

VOL II

Army Form C. 2118.

WAR DIARY
or
INTELLIGENCE SUMMARY.
(Erase heading not required.)

Place	Date	Hour	Summary of Events and Information	Remarks and references to Appendices
GODEWAERSVELDT	1/9/17		Moved by motor lorries from GODEWAERSVELDT to BAILLEU	
BAILLEU	2/9/17 to 5/9/17		General Fatigues	
	6/9/17		Moved by motor lorries to NEUVE EGLISE	
NEUVE EGLISE	7/9/17		General Fatigues	
	8/9/17		Moved by motor lorries to NIEPPE	
NIEPPE	9/9/17 to 12/9/17		General Fatigues	
	13/9/17 to 24/9/17		Getting camouflage material into position & erecting camouflage	
	24/9/17		No 98535 Gr Taylor slightly wounded on the 20/9/17. Since returned to duty.	
	25/9/17 to 30/9/17		Supplying men to assist X Battery preparing gun positions	

Approach Lt. RFA
OC 2/8 T.M.Bty

Army Form C. 2118

WAR DIARY
or
INTELLIGENCE SUMMARY.
(Erase heading not required.)

Confidential

WAR DIARY
W/8 HEAVY TRENCH MORTAR BTY.
SEPTEMBER
VOL II

Army Form C. 2118.

WAR DIARY
or
INTELLIGENCE SUMMARY.
(Erase heading not required.)

Place	Date	Hour	Summary of Events and Information	Remarks and references to Appendices
Godewaersvelde	1/9/17		Moved by motor lorries from Godewaersvelde to Bailleul	
Bailleul	2/9/17	6pm	General fatigues. On the 7th moved to Neuve Eglise by lorries	
Neuve Eglise	7/9/17–9/9/17		General fatigues	
Neippe	9/9/17–12/9/17		Moved on the 9th to Neippe. General fatigues	
	12/9/17– 30/9/17		Started work on gun position in right section on 14th. Battery was employed on this job for two weeks. Found carrying parties for other batteries. Pit completed and 1 gun installed ready for firing on the 30th. On the 6th 2nd Lt Statham rejoined battery from 3rd Battery R.F.A. On the 7th Capt Brown left battery to act as D.T.M.O in letters above to _____. On the 10th 2nd Lt Drake rejoined battery from 35th Battery R.F.A.	

A.P. Statham
2nd Lt R.F.A
W/15 T.M.B

Army Form C. 2118.

Vol 17

C.W. Haskins Lt.
X/8 T.M.B.

WAR DIARY
or
INTELLIGENCE SUMMARY.
(Erase heading not required.)

WAR-DIARY

OF

X/8 Trench. Mortar. Battery

From 1/10/17 To 31/10/17

Vol II

WAR DIARY
or
INTELLIGENCE SUMMARY.
(Erase heading not required.)

Army Form C. 2118.

Place	Date	Hour	Summary of Events and Information	Remarks and references to Appendices
NIEPPE	1/10/17		A Party of one N.C.O. + 4 men proceed to the line, Map Ref C.1.d 10.85. 10 Pounds retired from the 6" Newton Mortar at the Range 8x0' on Enemy C.5.d Enemy retaliated strongly with 4-2 gas shell.	
	2/10/17		One man proceed to the line with rations. No 915488 Gun: Morang. F.F.A. wounded in action. 10 Rounds was fired from the 6" Newton Mortar from C.1.d 10.85 on enemy position C.5.d Enemy very active on our quarters.	
	3/10/17		One man proceed to the line with rations. Remainder billet fatigues etc.	
	4/10/17		Party of one N.C.O + 4 men proceed to the line. Remainder billet fatigues.	
	5/10/17		Commanding officer proceed to the line to plan out a new position for 6" Newton Mortar Map Ref C.10.d 10.25 One man proceed to the line with rations. Remainder Parade for Baths.	
	6/10/17		General fatigues etc in Billet.	
	7/10/17		Ditto	
	8/10/17		Ditto	
	9/10/17		2 N.C.O. and 8 men parade for baths	
	10/10/17		One N.C.O + 2 men proceed to the Coal Dump & draw coal for mediums & any Batteries Remainder fatigues in billet.	
	11/10/17		1 N.C.O + 5 men proceed to the line and prepare a new emplacement for 6" M.M. Map Ref C.10.d.1025.	

WAR DIARY
or
INTELLIGENCE SUMMARY.
(Erase heading not required.)

Army Form C. 2118.

Place	Date	Hour	Summary of Events and Information	Remarks and references to Appendices
NIEPPE	12/10/17		One man proceed to the line with Rations. Lieut C.H Hastens R.F.A O.C. proceeds on a short leave to United Kingdom. Lieut A J Williams R.Q.A 3/B L/130y takes command of the battery.	
	13/10/17		Lieut A J Williams proceeds to the line is superintends the work of the L/M.M implement	
	14/10/17		Relief party of 1 N.C.O + 4 men proceed to the line. Remainder parade for baths	
	15/10/17		One man proceed to the line with ration remainder fatigues etc	
	16/10/17		Relief party of 1 N.C.O + 4 men proceed to the line. remainder billets fatigues	
	17/10/17		One man proceed to the line with ration Ditto	
	18/10/17-19/10/17		Relief party of 1 N.C.O + 4 men proceed to the line with ration	
	20/10/17		One man proceed to the line with Rations. remainder parade for baths	
	21/10/17		Ditto	
	22/10/17		Remainder General fatigue	
	23/10/17		Relief party of 1 N.C.O + 4 men proceed to the line with ration Remainder fatigue	
	24/10/17-25/10/17		One man proceed to the line with ration. General Fatigue in billet	
	26/10/17		General Fatigue in billet	
	27/10/17		Inspection of the battery by the A.D L/M.O	
	28/10/17		Battery parade for church	

Army Form C. 2118.

WAR DIARY
or
INTELLIGENCE SUMMARY.
(Erase heading not required.)

Place	Date	Hour	Summary of Events and Information	Remarks and references to Appendices
NIEPPE	29/10/19		One N.C.O + 5 men proceed to the line remainder fatigues in billet	
	30/10/19		One N.C.O + 2 men proceed to mobile workshop with a 6" newton mortar one man with the assistance of 3 men from 2/87 m/b ty proceed to the line and bring out one 6" newton gun to seven tree avenue which was pick up by G.S. Wagon and brought back to billet	
	31/10/19		The battery was inspected by the C.R.A. 8th Div.	

Army Form C. 2118.

WAR DIARY
or
INTELLIGENCE SUMMARY.

War Diary

of

Y/8 Trench Mortar B<u>t</u>y

From 1/10/17
To 31/10/17

Vol II

WAR DIARY or INTELLIGENCE SUMMARY

Army Form C. 2118.

Place	Date	Hour	Summary of Events and Information	Remarks and references to Appendices
NIEPPE	1/10/17 To		Bty in the line working on Gun positions & dugouts.	
			Work was carried out under great difficulties, hostile flying F.A's constantly passing over line	
	11/10/17		On the 14/10/17 D.T.M.O + O/C visited Brigade Major at the Brigade & were ordered to prepare 2 2" T.M's positions for wire cutting at U.11.D.90.70 and U.18.A.28.30. Both of these	
	15/10/17		positions were found to be impossible.	
			Reconnoitred La Bassé Ville with O.T.M.O.	
	12/10/17		One Officer + one other Rank to 4th Army School of Mortars undergoing 6" Newton T.M course	
	15/10/17		Two N.C.O & 7 men to 2nd Army School of Mortars undergoing 6" Newton T.M course	
	17/10/17		Personnel withdrawn from the line	
	18/10/17		Reconnoitred infantry out post at x y z.	
	17/10/17 To		27/10/17 One Officer + one other Rank returned from 4th Army School of Mortars	
	29/10/17		Parades. Fatigues etc. Eight other Rank returned from 2nd Army School of Mortars	
	30/10/17		Prepared gun positions for demonstration on 6" Newton T.M for Divisional Staff	
	31/10/17		C.R.A's inspection	

J.J Stent
O/C 9/6 T.M.B

Army Form C. 2118.

WAR DIARY
or
INTELLIGENCE SUMMARY.

(Erase heading not required.)

CONFIDENTIAL.

WAR DIARY.
OF
Z/8 TRENCH MORTAR BATTERY

FROM 1/10/17 to 31/10/17

VOL II

Army Form C. 2118.

WAR DIARY
or
INTELLIGENCE SUMMARY.
(Erase heading not required.)

Instructions regarding War Diaries and Intelligence Summaries are contained in F.S. Regs., Part II. and the Staff Manual respectively. Title pages will be prepared in manuscript.

Place	Date	Hour	Summary of Events and Information	Remarks and references to Appendices
NIEPPE	1/10/17 to 10/10/17		Battery in the line working on gun emplacements for Y/8 T.M.Bty. Owing to low flying E.A. constantly crossing our line, work was carried out under great difficulties.	
	11/10/17		Personnel withdrawn from the line.	
	12/10/17		10 other ranks proceeded to IV Army School of Mortars for instructions on 6" Newton T.M.	
	15/10/17		3 other ranks proceeded to II Army School of Mortars for instructions on 6" Newton T.M.	
	16/10/17 to 28/10/17		Parades, fatigues, Etc.	
	28-10-17		9 ORs returned from IV Army School of Mortars	
	29-10-17		3 ORs returned from II Army School of Mortars.	
	30/10/17 31/10/17		Parades, and making gun emplacement for 6" Newton T.M. demonstration	A. Vincent Lieut. O.C. 7/8 T.M.By

Army Form C. 2118.

WAR DIARY
or
INTELLIGENCE SUMMARY.

(Erase heading not required.)

Confidential

WAR DIARY

of Heavy Trench Mortar Battery

20/8

From 1-10-17 to

VOL II

WAR DIARY
or
INTELLIGENCE SUMMARY.
(Erase heading not required.)

Army Form C. 2118.

Place	Date	Hour	Summary of Events and Information	Remarks and references to Appendices
PLOEGSTEERT	1-7.1.10/17		Position on right sector completed (CAA to 47) ton/sectors ammunition dress made and gun ready for fit up	
	7-21/10/17		Position on left sector (48 to 54 invic) being made. Difficulties in construction of this position have been very large. In the place all numbers a subsec, gun etc had to be carried over 2000 yds: ground over here is supersaturated and approach to the position is under direct observation from WARNETON Tower.	
	9-31/10/17		Firing from position on night On attempt at enemy places has been tried on various targets viz T.M. positions Mc emplacements and other strong points. Good results have been obtained. Enemy retaliated on field batteries & M.R. park two days when he has put outposition 5 with the position causing slight damage to 4.2" shells on the position b.r.	

31/10/17.

G.C.P. Notum
O/c 4/8 T.M. B.G.

HQ R.A.
8 Divn

TRENCH MORTAR
HEADQUARTERS,
8TH DIVL. ARTILLERY.
No. TM 281
Date

Herewith War
Diaries of 8 Div T
M B'ts for the Month
of November.

30-11-17.

S.L. Bobbon Lieut for Capt.
D.T.M.O 8 D.A.

Army Form C. 2118.

WAR DIARY
or
INTELLIGENCE SUMMARY.
(Erase heading not required.)

WAR — DIARY
OF
X/8 French Mortar Battery R.A.
From 17/11/17 to 30/11/17

Vol III

Army Form C. 2118.

WAR DIARY
or
INTELLIGENCE SUMMARY.
(Erase heading not required.)

Instructions regarding War Diaries and Intelligence Summaries are contained in F. S. Regs., Part II. and the Staff Manual respectively. Title pages will be prepared in manuscript.

Place	Date	Hour	Summary of Events and Information	Remarks and references to Appendices
NEIPPE	1-11-17		A party of one N.C.O and 4 men proceed to the line. Map Ref/ C.1.ª 10. 85. Remainder fatigues in Billet etc	
"	2-11-17		The battery clean up stores in General	
"	3-11-17		Battery parade for baths. Lieut A.E. Woods R.F.A granted a short leave to United Kingdom Lieut S.L. Bibby R.F.A attached from Y. & T.M. Btty and takes Command of the battery	
"	4-11-17		Relief party of one N.C.O and 4 men proceed to the line. Remainder fatigues in billets	
"	5-11-17		The battery clean up billets in General	
"	6-11-17 7-11-17		General fatigues in billets and clean up gun stores.	
"	8-11-17		Relief party of one N.C.O and 4 men proceed to the line, remainder parade for baths	
"	9-11-17		The detachment of one N.C.O and 4 men withdrawn from the line, one 6 M.M handed over to the 3.3rd Divisional Trench Mortars.	
New PPSN	10(11-17)		The battery move from NEIPPE by Motor Lorries to new area. Map Ref (H.16.C-20)	
"	11-11-17 12-11-17		6 men on fatigues officers mess. Remainder Camp fatigues	
"	13-11-17 26-11-17		Battery road making and Salving Guns	
"	27-11-17 28-11-17		Salving Ammunition. And repairing dug-outs near Passchendaele Ridge	
"	29-11-17 30-11-17		Salving Guns and Ammunition.	

H. Bolton Lieut
OC. X/17 T.M.B.

2353 Wt. W2544/1454 700,000 5/15 D.D.&L. A.D.S.S./Forms/C. 2118.

APPENDIX IX.

8th DIVISIONAL ARTILLERY.

CASUALTIES that have occurred in Personnel during Month ending November, 1917.

	33rd Brigade R.F.A.		45th Brigade R.F.A.		8th D.A.C.		Trench Mortars.	
	Officers.	O.R.	Officers.	O.R.	Officers.	O.R.	Officers.	O.R.
Strength on 1st	—	—	—	—	—	—	2	23
SICK.	—	—	—	—	—	—	1	nil
KILLED.	—	—	—	—	—	—	nil	nil
*WOUNDED. AT DUTY.	—	—	—	—	—	—	nil	nil*
INJURED.	—	—	—	—	—	—	nil	nil
MISSING.	—	—	—	—	—	—	nil	nil
ABSENTEES.	—	—	—	—	—	—	nil	nil
TOTAL WASTAGE.	—	—	—	—	—	—	1	nil
Re-inforcements received.	—	—	—	—	—	—	1	nil
STRENGTH AT END OF MONTH.	—	—	—	—	—	—	2	23

S. Bibby
OC ⅔ Lieut. R.F.A.
T.M. 13ᵗʰʸ R.A.

Army Form C. 2118.

WAR DIARY
or
INTELLIGENCE SUMMARY.
(Erase heading not required.)

WAR DIARY

OF

Y/8 TRENCH MORTAR BY

FROM

1-11-1917 TO 30-11-1917

Vol II

WAR DIARY
or
INTELLIGENCE SUMMARY.
(Erase heading not required.)

Army Form C. 2118.

Place	Date	Hour	Summary of Events and Information	Remarks and references to Appendices
NIEPPE	1/11/17		Parade 26½: Guns withdrawn from the line 5/11/17	
	9/11/17 to		The centre of the Division of about was relieved by 66th Div. gun positions	
			to hand over to H.Q. 2nd Division	
	10/11/17		Preceded by order Series 6 H.Q. 6.R.F.C.	
KRUISTRAAT AREA	11/11/17 & 12/11/17		Fatigues Etc.	
	13/11/17 to			
	17/11/17		Road mending for the 3rd Bde R.F.A. & assisting The 6 new guns forward	
	19/11/17 to		Assisting 5th, 55th + 57th Bdys. R.F.A. to move guns forward (casualties on 19/11/17 2 wounded at shelf.)	
	23/11/17			
	24/11/17		Parades Church Parade 25/11/17	
	25/11/17			
	26/11/17 to		Salving Guns & Ammunition	
	30/11/17			

A. Stewart? R.F.A.
O.C. 46 T.M.B.

8th DIVISIONAL ARTILLERY.

APPENDIX.

CASUALTIES that have occurred in Personnel during Month ending November.

	33rd Brigade R.F.A.		45th Brigade R.F.A.		8th D.A.C.		Trench Mortars.	
	Officers.	O.R.	Officers.	O.R.	Officers.	O.R.	Officers.	O.R.
Strength on 1st							2	23
SICK.							Nil	Nil
KILLED.							Nil	Nil
WOUNDED.							Nil	2 (at duty)
INJURED.							Nil	Nil
MISSING.							Nil	Nil
ABSENTEES.							Nil	Nil
TOTAL WASTAGE.							Nil	1
Re-inforcements received.							Nil	Nil
STRENGTH AT END OF MONTH.							2	22

A. Stead Lieut. R.F.A.
O.C. V/8 T.M.By.

Army Form C. 2118.

WAR DIARY
or
INTELLIGENCE SUMMARY.
(Erase heading not required.)

CONFIDENTIAL

WAR DIARY

OF

Z/8 TRENCH MORTAR BTY

From 1-11-1917 to 30-11-1917

VOL II

Army Form C. 2118.

WAR DIARY
or
INTELLIGENCE SUMMARY.
(Erase heading not required.)

Instructions regarding War Diaries and Intelligence Summaries are contained in F. S. Regs., Part II. and the Staff Manual respectively. Title pages will be prepared in manuscript.

Place	Date	Hour	Summary of Events and Information	Remarks and references to Appendices
NIEPPE.	1-11-17 to 9-11-17		Parades, fatigues, etc.	
	10-11-17		Moved by Motor lorries to Canadian T.M. Camp. H.16.c.2.0	
KRUSSTRAAT AREA	11-11-17 to 12-11-17		Fatigues and improving the Camp.	
	13-11-17 to 17-8-17		Road making & assisting 3rd Bty to move guns to forward positions	
	18-11-17 to 23-11-17		Salving guns in the forward area. Lt Parker & Lt Brown slightly wounded 19-11-17.	
	24-11-17		Parades Fatigues etc	
	25-11-17			
	26-11-17 to 30-11-17		Salving Guns & Ammunition in the forward area.	

E.M.Brown Capt.
for O.C. 7x/8 T.M.Bte

2/8 Trench Mortar Bty.

8th DIVISIONAL ARTILLERY.

APPENDIX.

CASUALTIES that have occurred in Personnel during Month ending 30th November.

	33rd Brigade R.F.A.		45th Brigade R.F.A.		8th D.A.C.		Trench Mortars	
	Officers.	O.R.	Officers.	O.R.	Officers.	C.R.	Officers.	O.R.
Strength on 1st							3	23
SICK.							-	3
KILLED.							-	-
WOUNDED.							1	1
TRANSFERRED								
INJURED.							1	-
Reposted to 8th DAC								1
MISSING							-	-
ABSENTEES.							-	-
TOTAL WASTAGE.							2	5
Re-inforcements received.							-	1
STRENGTH AT END OF MONTH.							1	19

for OC 2/8 T.M. Bty.

Army Form C. 2118.

WAR DIARY
or
INTELLIGENCE SUMMARY.
(Erase heading not required.)

Confidential

War Diary

of

V/6 Heavy Trench Mortar Battery

From 1-11-17 To 30-11-17

VOL II

WAR DIARY or INTELLIGENCE SUMMARY

Army Form C. 2118.

Place	Date	Hour	Summary of Events and Information	Remarks and references to Appendices
Lat 4	1-11-14		Extra party sent to Left sector position to prevent progress of Germ O.P. Right sector 2 men in charge	
	2-11-14		No firing on Right sector Left sector continuing with entrenchment	
	3-11-14		Left sector. Still continuing entrenchment Right sector no firing	
	4-11-14		Large party recalled from AS Left sector Right sector no firing	
	5-11-14		Left sector situation unaltered. Snipers over all party raided two guns	
	6-11-14		No firing Right sector 2 men accidentally turned by explosion of 4·5 mine on fuselage of all British Right sector snipers busy firing	
	7-11-14		Observations made all hands. Mushing bill to Right Sector No firing	
	8-11-14		Lt. Inspector Peperantu & C.A. Helmet Inspector General Latripes left camp Right sector	
	9-11-14		Inspection prince General Latripes Inst. Hale France Hermon. Rail G.M.T forces	
	10-11-14		Move to new area Inf. Lunes 9am arrive new area 10am British position handed over	
	11-11-14		Inspection General Latripes blessing Band Departs to etc.	
	12-11-14		Party of 15 men to A.R.P. Party of 15 men for Lieut Groner Florent General Latripes	
	13-11-14		2 Parties of 15 men Road Work 15 men for G.R.P 19 22 Party Road Work 6 men 5 men Dynm	
	14-11-14		Road Work Parade 3.30, 5 men Dyr'n & R.E.O reconnoitering the road General Latripes	

WAR DIARY
or
INTELLIGENCE SUMMARY.
(Erase heading not required.)

Army Form C. 2118.

Instructions regarding War Diaries and Intelligence Summaries are contained in F. S. Regs., Part II. and the Staff Manual respectively. Title pages will be prepared in manuscript.

Place	Date	Hour	Summary of Events and Information	Remarks and references to Appendices
	15-11-17		Party Parade for Salvaging 3-30ᵃᵐ 30 men 40 500 men General Fatigues	
	18-11-17		Party Salving Parade 3-30ᵃᵐ General Fatigues Bathing Parade 12-45ᵃᵐ	
	19-11-17 20-11-17		Parties Salving Parade and General Fatigues for the Rest	
	21-11-17		Party Salving Parade and Inspection of General Fatigues	
	22-11-17 23-11-17		Salving Party 4ᵃᵐ parade, Fatigues for the Rest	
	24-11-17		Party for A&L5s 9am the rest inspection Parade 2pm Inspection of kit	
	25-11-17		Party for Line Party 6-30ᵃᵐ A&L5s General Fatigues and Inspection of the rest	
	26-11-17		Party for Line Salving Parade 8-30ᵃᵐ Party 5 men 10ᵗᵒⁿ Inspection General Fatigues	
	27-11-17		Salving Party to Line Parade 8-45ᵃᵐ Party 8 men A&L 5s Inspection General Fatigues	
	28-11-17		Party for Salving Parade 3-30ᵃᵐ Party for A&L5s 5 men Bathing Parade 1-45ᵃᵐ	
	29-11-17		Parade for Salving Party 4ᵃᵐ A&L 5s party 5 men Inspection and Cleaning Guns	
	30-11-17		Line Party for Salving Parade 7-30ᵃᵐ 6 men A&L 5s the rest General Fatigues	

H. Robertson 2/Lt P.F.A.

8th DIVISIONAL ARTILLERY.

CASUALTIES that have occurred in Personnel during month ending ....November....

	33rd Brigade R.F.A.		45th Brigade R.F.A.		8th D.A.C.		Trench Mortars.	
	Officers.	O.R.	Officers.	O.R.	Officers.	O.R.	Officers.	O.R.
Strength on 1st							3	61
SICK.							Nil *4 Brig. has not returned yet*	Nil
KILLED.							Nil	Nil
WOUNDED.							Nil	2
INJURED.							Nil	Nil
MISSING.							Nil	Nil
ABSENTEES.							Nil	Nil
TOTAL WASTAGE.							Nil	1
Re-inforcements received.							1	Nil
STRENGTH AT END OF MONTH.							4	58

A.R.Adams Capt. R.F.A.
Cmdg. T.M. Batteries 8th Div.

Army Form C. 2118.

WAR DIARY
or
INTELLIGENCE SUMMARY.
(Erase heading not required.)

WAR-DIARY

OF

X/8 French Mortar Battery R.A

FROM 1-12-17. To 31-12-17

Vol III

Army Form C. 2118.

WAR DIARY
or
INTELLIGENCE SUMMARY.
(Erase heading not required.)

Instructions regarding War Diaries and Intelligence Summaries are contained in F. S. Regs., Part II. and the Staff Manual respectively. Title pages will be prepared in manuscript.

Place	Date	Hour	Summary of Events and Information	Remarks and references to Appendices
KRUYSTRAAT AREA H.16.5-20	1/12/17		The battery clean up camp in general &c.	
	2/12/17		Five men assisting to make advance gun emplacement for the 5th Battery R.F.A. remainder fatigues in camp	
	3/12/17		Two N.C.O's and 3 men, carrying party for R.E. material making D.R's. Road making in the forward area.	
	4/12/17		Four men Road making in the forward area	
	5/12/17		Four men assist the R.E. in forward area remainder clean up in general	
	6/12/17		Four men assist 5th Battery to move guns to new position	
	7/12/17		Two men assist 55th Battery R.F.A. to move guns from own position	
Remainder	8/12/17		The battery move from camp H.16.6.20 to new area Vlamertinghe	
	9/12/17		Four men Road making for 3rd + 5th Battery R.F.A. in the forward area	
	10/12/17		Five men carrying timber to Bell Vue out post for R.E. in forward area	
	11/12/17		Six men carrying party for R.E. in forward area	
	12/12/17		Nine men assist R.E. to lay down light railway, and carrying ammunition for 55th Bty R.F.A.	
	13/12/17		Eight men making gun pits for the 31st battery R.F.A in forward area	
	14/12/17		The battery carried on physical training &c. must prepare guns for B.A.H.R.² & D.D.	
	15/12/17		Three men assisting the R.E's in forward area. Remainder to gym in billet	
	16/12/17			
	17/12/17			
	18/12/17			
	19/12/17			
	20/12/17			
	31/12/17			

APPENDIX IX.

8th DIVISIONAL ARTILLERY.

CASUALTIES that have occurred in Personnel during Month ending December 1917

	33rd Brigade R.F.A.		45th Brigade R.F.A.		8th D.A.C.		Trench Mortars.	
	Officers.	O.R.	Officers.	O.R.	Officers.	O.R.	Officers.	O.R.
Strength on 1st.	-	-	-	-	-	-	3	23
SICK.	-	-	-	-	-	-	one	nil
KILLED.	-	-	-	-	-	-	nil	nil
WOUNDED.	-	-	-	-	-	-	nil	nil
INJURED.	-	-	-	-	-	-	nil	nil
MISSING.	-	-	-	-	-	-	nil	nil
ABSENTEES.	-	-	-	-	-	-	nil	nil
TOTAL WASTAGE.	-	-	-	-	-	-	1	nil
Re-inforcements received.	-	-	-	-	-	-	nil	nil
STRENGTH AT END OF MONTH.	-	-	-	-	-	-	2	23

Howitzer or Trench X/8 T.M. Btty
J.Bailey

Army Form C. 2118.

WAR DIARY
or
INTELLIGENCE SUMMARY.
(Erase heading not required.)

Instructions regarding War Diaries and Intelligence Summaries are contained in F. S. Regs., Part II. and the Staff Manual respectively. Title pages will be prepared in manuscript.

Place	Date	Hour	Summary of Events and Information	Remarks and references to Appendices
			WAR DIARY.	
			OF	
			1/8 TRENCH MORTAR BTY	
			FROM	
			1-12-1917 To 31-12-1917	
			VOL II	

Army Form C. 2118.

WAR DIARY
or
INTELLIGENCE SUMMARY.
(Erase heading not required.)

Instructions regarding War Diaries and Intelligence Summaries are contained in F. S. Regs., Part II. and the Staff Manual respectively. Title pages will be prepared in manuscript.

Place	Date	Hour	Summary of Events and Information	Remarks and references to Appendices
KRUSTRAAT.	1/2/17		Salving guns at KANSAS CORNER.	
	2/2/17			
	3/2/17		Working under R.E.s constructing O.P. at BELLE VUE	
	4/2/17		Working at 5th By. R.F.A. Road making	
	5/2/17		Under R.E.s at BELLE VUE	
	6/2/17			
	7/2/17 to 9/2/17		Working at 5th & 55th By R.F.A. Gun lines	
VLAMERTINGHE	10/2/17		Bty moved to VLAMERTINGHE	
	11/2/17		Road making, 1st & 5th By R.F.A. Winnipeg X Roads.	
	12/2/17		Laying Railway under R.Es by R.F.A. By. Gun lines	
	13/2/17 to 14/2/17		Carrying up Ammunition L. 55th Bty R.F.A.	
	15/2/17			
	16/2/17 to 20/2/17		Salving Guns, D.T.m.s. L.Gun? ammunition & Rifles, to an Efwad ref named J am Troops.	
	21/2/17 to 28/2/17		Training Physical & blo.	

APPENDIX IX.

8th DIVISIONAL ARTILLERY. (Y/8 T.M.B'y')

CASUALTIES that have occurred in Personnel during Month ending December 1917.

	33rd Brigade R.F.A.		45th Brigade R.F.A.		8th D.A.C.		Trench Mortars.	
	Officers.	O.R.	Officers.	O.R.	Officers.	O.R.	Officers.	O.R.
Strength on 1st							2	22
SICK.							Nil	Nil
KILLED.							Nil	Nil
WOUNDED.							Nil	Nil
INJURED.							Nil	Nil
MISSING.							Nil	Nil
ABSENTEES.							Nil	Nil
TOTAL WASTAGE.							Nil	Nil
Re-inforcements received.							Nil	Nil
STRENGTH AT END OF MONTH.							2	22

Lieut. R.F.A.
O/C Y/8 T.M.B'y.

Army Form C. 2118.

WAR DIARY
or
INTELLIGENCE SUMMARY.
(Erase heading not required.)

CONFIDENTIAL

WAR DIARY.
OF
2/8 TRENCH MORTAR BATTERY.

From 1-12-17 to 31-12-17

VOL II

Army Form C. 2118.

WAR DIARY
or
INTELLIGENCE SUMMARY.
(Erase heading not required.)

Instructions regarding War Diaries and Intelligence Summaries are contained in F. S. Regs., Part II. and the Staff Manual respectively. Title pages will be prepared in manuscript.

Place	Date	Hour	Summary of Events and Information	Remarks and references to Appendices
KRUISSTRAHT AREA	1-12-17		5 ORs attached to 39th DAG at Corps Gun Post. Remainder of Battery on fatigues.	
	2-12-17		Battery assisting 5th Battery RGA to make alterations of junction/Improvements.	
	3-12-17		Carrying timber for RE's to BELLE VUE outpost	
	4-12-17		Road making in forward area	
	5-12-17		" "	
	6-12-17		Carrying timber for RE's to BELLE VUE outpost	
	7-12-17		Assisting 5th Battery to more guns from their positions	
	8-12-17		" "	
	9-12-17		Assisting 5.5" Battery to move guns from their positions	
	10-12-17		Moved by RA Waggons from Camp at Hill c 20 to billets in VLAMERTINGHE	
VLAMERTINGHE	11-12-17		Road making for 3rd & 5" Battery	
	12-12-17		Carrying timber etc for RE's to BELLE VUE outpost	
	13-12-17		Laying down railway materials under RE's to battery positions	
	14-12-17		Moving guns from positions of 5.5 BG	
	15-12-17		" "	
	16-12-17		Moving guns	
	17-12-17		Moving guns from positions of 52 d RGA	

(A583) Wt. W807/M1072 359,000 4/17 Sch. 52a Forms/C/2118/14
D. D. & L., London, E.C.

WAR DIARY
or
INTELLIGENCE SUMMARY.

Army Form C. 2118.

Place	Date	Hour	Summary of Events and Information	Remarks and references to Appendices
VLAMERTINGHE	18-12-17		history of 53rd Trg/position	
	19-12-17			
	30-12-17		framing & Physical etc	
	31-12-17		3.6Bde proceeded to RHQs for writing up	

H March Lt REA
DO 3/4 TM Bty

APPENDIX.

8th DIVISIONAL ARTILLERY.

CASUALTIES that have occurred in Personnel during Month ending 31st Dec. ... in 2/8 T.M. Bty

	33rd Brigade R.F.A.		45th Brigade R.F.A.		8th D.A.C.		Trench Mortars.	
	Officers.	O.R.	Officers.	O.R.	Officers.	O.R.	Officers.	O.R.
Strength on 1st							2	19
SICK.							Nil	Nil
KILLED.							Nil	Nil
WOUNDED.							Nil	Nil
INJURED.							Nil	Nil
MISSING.							Nil	Nil
ABSENTEES.							Nil	Nil
TOTAL WASTAGE.							Nil	Nil
Re-inforcements received.							Nil	1
STRENGTH AT END OF MONTH.							2	20

Aylward Lieut. RFA
OC 2/8 Trench Mortar Bty

Army Form C. 2118

WAR DIARY
or
INTELLIGENCE SUMMARY
(Erase heading not required.)

Confidential

War Diary
of
10/8 Trench Mortar Battery

From 1-12-17 to 31-12-17. 1917

Vol II

WAR DIARY
or
INTELLIGENCE SUMMARY.
(Erase heading not required.)

Army Form C. 2118.

Instructions regarding War Diaries and Intelligence Summaries are contained in F. S. Regs., Part II. and the Staff Manual respectively. Title pages will be prepared in manuscript.

Place	Date	Hour	Summary of Events and Information	Remarks and references to Appendices
	1/12/17		Party of 11 men & one N.C.O to the Lon. Gen. Hosp. on fatigue	
	2/12/17		and 1 N.C.O. & 4 men for H.Q. Div. Arty. Host. Gen. fatigue. Party of 15 men & one N.C.O to the Lon. Gen. Palace 1. N.C.O. & 4 men for H.Q. Div. Arty. and 1 N.C.O & 4 men to A.R.P. H.Q. coal General fatigues	
	3/12/17		Party of 3 N.C.O's and 7 men to Lon. Palace party of 1 N.C.O & 4 men for H.Q. Div. Arty. Gen. Hosp fatigue	
	4/12/17		Party of 1 N.C.O & 11 men for the Lon. Palace party of 1 N.C.O & 4 men for H.Q. Div. Arty. at fatigue	
	5/12/17		Party of 1 N.C.O & 5 men for Lon. Party of 1 N.C.O & 4 men for H.Q. Div. Arty. the ord. 1 Ord N.C.O. and Serg. fatigues	
	6/12/17		Party of 2 N.C.O's & 8 men for the Lon. Palace Party 1 N.C.O & 4 men for H.Q. Div. Arty. ill most supplying of Box. Regimental & fatigues	
	7/12/17		Party of 2 N.C.O's 18 men for Lon. Gen. Palace not fatigue.	
	8/12/17		Party of 1 N.C.O 10 men for Lon. G. Hosp. on fatigue	

Army Form C. 2118.

WAR DIARY
or
INTELLIGENCE SUMMARY.
(Erase heading not required.)

Instructions regarding War Diaries and Intelligence Summaries are contained in F. S. Regs., Part II. and the Staff Manual respectively. Title pages will be prepared in manuscript.

Place	Date	Hour	Summary of Events and Information	Remarks and references to Appendices
	9.12.17		Party of 1 N.C.O. & 3 men for H.Q. Gen. Fatigue	
	10.12.17		The rest of Bn. on General Fatigues. Moved to new area.	
	11.12.17		Party of 3 N.C.O's & 10 men for H.Q. Fatigue	
	12.12.17		Party of 1 N.C.O. & 9 men for H.Q. Fatigue	
	13.12.17		Party of 4 N.C.O. & 10 men for H.Q. Fatigue	
	14.12.17		Party of 2 N.C.O. & 13 men for H.Q. Gen. Fatigue. 20 men	
	15.12.17		Head of 2 Bn. Party of 2 N.C.O. & 7 men for H.Q. Gen. Fatigue. 20 men for Bath. Bn. on 1 General Fatigue	
	16.12.17		1 N.C.O. & 10 men for the Len. H.Q. Gen. Fatigue. Bn. on 1 Gen. Fatigue	
	17.12.17		3 N.C.O.'s & 7 men for H.Q. Len. Gen. Fatigue	
	18.12.17		Party of 1 N.C.O. & 11 men for H.Q. Len. Gen. Fatigue next Gen. Fatigue	
	19.12.17		Party of 3 men for Guard at H.Q. Div Arty. Knees Len. Fatigue	
	20.12.17		Party of 3 men for Guard at H.Q. Div Arty. Knees Len. Fatigue	
	21.12.17		Party of 3 men for Guard at H.Q. Div Arty. Knees Len. Fatigue	

Army Form C. 2118

WAR DIARY
or
INTELLIGENCE SUMMARY
(Erase heading not required.)

Instructions regarding War Diaries and Intelligence Summaries are contained in F. S. Regs., Part II. and the Staff Manual respectively. Title Pages will be prepared in manuscript.

Place	Date	Hour	Summary of Events and Information	Remarks and references to Appendices
	22.12.17		Party of 3 men for Guard at HQ Div Arty. The Rest Inspection Fatigues	
	23.12.17		Do. Do.	
	24.12.17		Do. Do.	
	25.12.17		1 N.C.O. & 9 men returned from Guard of A.R.P.a	
	26.12.17		Party of 3 men for Guard at H.Q Div Arty Rest Inspection Fatigue	
	27.12.17		" Do. Do.	
	28.12.17		" Do. Do.	
	29.12.17		1 Physical Exercises	
			Party of 3 men for Guard at H.Q Div Arty. The rest Inspection and Physical Exercises	
	30.12.17		Inspection of Box Respirator, H.P Helmet and Tin Hat. Presentation of Parchment Certificates to Cpl. Mee & Bom. Craven.	
	31.12.17		Party of 15 men for 250 Tunneling Company	

R. A. Hawkins, 2 Lieut.
R.F.A.

APPENDIX.

8th DIVISIONAL ARTILLERY.

CASUALTIES that have occurred in Personnel during Month ending December ...5-12-17

	33rd Brigade R.F.A.		45th Brigade R.F.A.		8th D.A.C.		Trench Mortars.	
	Officers.	O.R.	Officers.	O.R.	Officers.	O.R.	Officers.	O.R.
Strength on 1st							3	65
SICK.							Nil	Nil
KILLED.							Nil	Nil
WOUNDED.							Nil	Nil
INJURED.							Nil	Nil
MISSING.							Nil	Nil
ABSENTEES.							Nil	Nil
TOTAL WASTAGE.							Nil	5
Re-inforcements received.							Nil	Nil
STRENGTH AT END OF MONTH.							3	66

APPENDIX IX.

8th DIVISIONAL ARTILLERY.

CASUALTIES that have occurred in Personnel during Month ending ....

	33rd Brigade R.F.A.		45th Brigade R.F.A.		8th D.A.C.	
	Officers.	O.R.	Officers.	O.R.	Officers.	O.R.
Strength on 1st					3	
SICK.					Nil	
KILLED.					Nil	
WOUNDED.					Nil	
INJURED.					Nil	
MISSING.						
ABSENTEES.						
TOTAL WASTAGE.						
Re-inforcements received.						
STRENGTH AT END OF MONTH.						

Army Form C. 2118.

WAR DIARY
or
INTELLIGENCE SUMMARY.
(Erase heading not required.)

YM 20

WAR DIARY
OF
1/8 TRENCH MORTAR BY.
FROM
1-1-1918 TO 31-1-1918
VOL III

Army Form C. 2118.

WAR DIARY
or
INTELLIGENCE SUMMARY.
(Erase heading not required.)

Instructions regarding War Diaries and Intelligence Summaries are contained in F. S. Regs., Part II. and the Staff Manual respectively. Title pages will be prepared in manuscript.

Place	Date	Hour	Summary of Events and Information	Remarks and references to Appendices
VLAMERTINGHE	1/1/18		Parades &c.	
	2/1/18		Building reserve gun positions in the St Julien area for the 115th Brigade R.F.A.	
	3/1/18	10.30/1/18	Working under the 215th Coy R.E.s tunnelling at BELLE VIEW	R A
			Constructing 6" Mortar T.M. positions at BELLE VIEW	J.P. Stewart Lieut. O.C. 1/15 T.M. B?
	21/1/18		Moved into billets at Poperinghe	
PAPERINGHE	22/1/18	30/1/18	Guarding reserve gun positions in the Wietje & St Julien area	
			2nd Lieut M.S. Wood, R.F.A. Awarded Parchment Certificate by Divisional Commander Jan 6th "A"	
			No. 78773 Bd? L'Hope R.H.A. awarded Parchment Certificate by Divisional Commander Jan 6th 18 for gallantry & devotion to duty near PASSCHENDAELE & VLAMERTINGHE between 1st + 3rd December 1917. (D.R.O. A/64/1/17)	
			28578 Sgt R. Payne R.G.A. Awarded M.M. by Corps Commander Jan 4th 18 Gallery in action in front of YPRES Dec 18th 1917. Auth: VIII Corps "A" A.39 A/4/1/17	

APPENDIX.

8th DIVISIONAL ARTILLERY.

CASUALTIES that have occurred in Personnel during Month ending January 1918.

	33rd Brigade R.F.A.		45th Brigade R.F.A.		8th D.A.C.		Trench Mortars.	
	Officers.	O.R.	Officers.	O.R.	Officers.	O.R.	Officers.	O.R.
Strength on 1st							2	22
SICK.							Nil	Nil
KILLED.							Nil	Nil
WOUNDED.							Nil	Nil
INJURED.							Nil	Nil
MISSING.							Nil	Nil
ABSENTEES.							Nil	Nil
TOTAL WASTAGE.							Nil	Nil
Re-inforcements received.							Nil	Nil
STRENGTH AT END OF MONTH.							2	22

A. Steuny
Lieut. R.F.A.
O.C. 8/8 T.M. B'dy

Army Form C. 2118.

WAR DIARY
or
INTELLIGENCE SUMMARY.
(Erase heading not required.)

CONFIDENTIAL

WAR DIARY.

OF

Z/8 TRENCH MORTAR BTY

1-1-18 to 31-1-18.

VOL III

Army Form C. 2118.

WAR DIARY
or
INTELLIGENCE SUMMARY.
(Erase heading not required.)

Place	Date	Hour	Summary of Events and Information	Remarks and references to Appendices
FLAMERTINGHE	1-1-18		Parcus Physical Training etc	
	2-1-18			
	3-1-18		Making winter 18 pdr gun emplacements near St Julien for the 115th Bde RFA.	
	to			
	20-1-18		Working for the 215th Siege Battery R.G.A. during construction of Belle Vue — making sealing 6" howitzer gun emplacements on BELLE VUE	
POPERINGHE	21-1-18		Battery moved to billets at POPERINGHE. Guarding seven 18 pdr gun emplacements in the WIELTJE +	
	to			
	31-1-18		St JULIEN area. On 4th Lt AG Meek + Cpl Gornard R.H MM awarded the Parchment Certificate by GOC for gallantry + devotion to duty.	

A Woorch Lieut RMR4
OC 2/1x RMR4

8th DIVISIONAL ARTILLERY.   APPENDIX.

CASUALTIES that have occurred in Personnel during Month ending 31st January

	33rd Brigade R.F.A.		45th Brigade R.F.A.		8th D.A.C.		Trench Mortars.	
	Officers.	O.R.	Officers.	O.R.	Officers.	O.R.	Officers.	O.R.
Strength on 1st							1	20
SICK.							Nil	Nil
KILLED.							Nil	Nil
WOUNDED.							Nil	Nil
INJURED.							Nil	Nil
MISSING.							Nil	Nil
ABSENTEES.							Nil	Nil
TOTAL WASTAGE.							Nil	Nil
Re-inforcements received.							Nil	1
STRENGTH AT END OF MONTH.							1	21

Allworth
OC 2/8 TM Bty

Army Form C. 2118.

WAR DIARY
or
INTELLIGENCE SUMMARY.
(Erase heading not required.)

WAR-DIARY

OF

X/8 Trench Mortar Battery R.A.

FROM 1-1-18 TO 31-1-18

Vol III

[signature] 2nd Lt R.F.A.
O/c X/8 T.M. Battery

WAR DIARY
or
INTELLIGENCE SUMMARY.
(Erase heading not required.)

Army Form C. 2118.

Instructions regarding War Diaries and Intelligence Summaries are contained in F. S. Regs., Part II and the Staff Manual respectively. Title pages will be prepared in manuscript.

Place	Date	Hour	Summary of Events and Information	Remarks and references to Appendices
Hamurtinge	1/1/18	—	Physical Exercise and NCO's Lecture by the D.T.M.O 8th Div	
	2/1/18	—	General Fatigues in billets etc.	
	3/1/18	—	4 O.R.s assist in salving field guns in forward areas	
	4/1/18	—	General Fatigue in billets etc	
	5/1/18	—	The battery clean up guns stores etc	
	6/1/18	—	The battery Parade for baths. General Fatigues etc	
	7/1/18	—	2 O.R.'s with others from Y.Z & 8 T.M.Btys proceed to the line to prepare 6" N.M. implacements	
	8/1/18	—	General Fatigues in billets etc	
	9/1/18	—	1 N.C.O + 2 men with others from Y.Z & 8 T.M.Btys proceed to the line to prepare 6" N.M. implacements	
	10/1/18	—	General Fatigues in billets etc	
	11/1/18	—	2 O.R's with others from Y.Z & 8 T.M.Btys proceed to the line to prepare 6" N.M. implacements	
	12/1/18	—	General Fatigues, battery parade for baths	
	13/1/18	—	Battery Parade. Reading out orders by the C.O. Battery clean up guns, stores etc	
	14/1/18	—	1 NCO + 2 men with others from Y.Z & 8 T.M.Bty proceed to the line to prepare 6" N.M. implacements	
	15/1/18	—	1 NCO + 4 men carrying 6" N.M. Ammunition to the 6" N.M. implacements	
	16/1/18	—	2 O.R's with others from Y.Z & 8 T.M.Bty proceed to the line to prepare 6" N.M. implacements	

Army Form C. 2118.

WAR DIARY
or
INTELLIGENCE SUMMARY.
(Erase heading not required.)

Instructions regarding War Diaries and Intelligence Summaries are contained in F. S. Regs., Part II and the Staff Manual respectively. Title pages will be prepared in manuscript.

Place	Date	Hour	Summary of Events and Information	Remarks and references to Appendices
Flamertinge	17/1/18	—	Battery Kit inspection by O.C.	
	18/1/18		2 O.R. with others from X,Y & Z.T.M.B.Y proceed to the line to prepare L.N.M. emplacements	
	19/1/18		The battery clean up guns, stores and billets	
	20/1/18		The battery parade for Church	
	21/1/18		The battery move from Flamertinge to new area Poperinghe	
POPERINGHE	22/1/18		Battery Parade to clean up the billets.	
	23/1/18		Battery parade for inspection of equipment and Gas Helmets by O.C.	
	24/1/18		Battery parade for baths. 1 N.C.O + 5 men guarding 18 pdr emplacements in forward area	
	25/1/18		General fatigues in billets	
	26/1/18		1 N.C.O + 4 men guarding 18 pdr emplacements in forward area.	
	27/1/18		General fatigues in billets	
	28/1/18		1 N.C.O + 3 men guarding 18 pdr emplacements in forward area.	
	29/1/18		General fatigues in billets	
	30/1/18		Ditto	
	31/1/18		Ditto	

APPENDIX.

8th DIVISIONAL ARTILLERY.

CASUALTIES that have occurred in Personnel during Month ending January 1918

	33rd Brigade R.F.A.		45th Brigade R.F.A.		8th D.A.C.		Trench Mortars.	
	Officers.	O.R.	Officers.	O.R.	Officers.	O.R.	Officers.	O.R.
Strength on 1st							2	23
SICK.							nil	nil
KILLED.							nil	nil
WOUNDED.							nil	nil
INJURED.							nil	nil
MISSING.							nil	nil
ABSENTEES.							nil	nil
TOTAL WASTAGE.							nil	nil
Re-inforcements received.							nil	nil
STRENGTH AT END OF MONTH.							nil	nil

X/8 T.M. Btty

[signature]
OC X/8TM/8th Divnl RFA

Army Form C. 2118.

WAR DIARY
or
INTELLIGENCE SUMMARY.
(Erase heading not required.)

(Confidential)

WAR DIARY
of
W/8 HEAVY TRENCH MORTAR BTY
from 1-1-18 to 31-1-18
VOL III

Army Form C. 2118.

WAR DIARY
or
INTELLIGENCE SUMMARY.
(Erase heading not required.)

Instructions regarding War Diaries and Intelligence Summaries are contained in F. S. Regs., Part II. and the Staff Manual respectively. Title pages will be prepared in manuscript.

Place	Date	Hour	Summary of Events and Information	Remarks and references to Appendices
	9.1.1918		Party of 6 men & 1 N.C.O. Paraded at 6.0 A.M. for the Lines. The Batt. Paraded at 10.0 A.M. for Inspection & General Fatigue.	
	10.1.18		Parade at 10.0 A.M. Inspection & General Fatigue.	
	11.1.18		Party of 6 men & 1 N.C.O. Paraded at 6.0 A.M. for the Line. The Bat. Paraded at 10.0 A.M. for Inspection & General Fatigue.	
	12.1.18		Parade at 10.0 A.M. for Inspection & General Fatigue.	
	13.1.18		do. 10.30 A.M. do.	
	14.1.18		do. 10.0 A.M. do.	
	15.1.18		Party of 12 men & 2 N.C.O.s Paraded at 5.17 A.M. for the Line. The Batt. Paraded at 10.0 A.M. for Inspection & General Fatigue.	
	16.1.18		Parade at 10.30 A.M. for Inspection & General Fatigue.	
	17.1.18		Parade at 10.0 A.M. for Inspection & General Fatigue. A Party of 8 men & 2 N.C.O.s Paraded at 11.30 A.M. to Report Adjutant at H.Q. Div. Arty.	
	18.1.18		Party of 8 men & 2 N.C.O.s Paraded at 6.30 A.M. to continue returns to Augment at H.Q. Div. Arty. Usual inspection & General Fatigue and	

Army Form C. 2118.

WAR DIARY
or
INTELLIGENCE SUMMARY.
(Erase heading not required.)

Instructions regarding War Diaries and Intelligence Summaries are contained in F. S. Regs., Part II. and the Staff Manual respectively. Title pages will be prepared in manuscript.

Place	Date	Hour	Summary of Events and Information	Remarks and references to Appendices
	1.1.1918		Parade 10.30 A.M. Inspection & General Fatigues.	
	2.1.18		Parade 10.0 A.M. Inspection, Physical Exercises & Gen. Fatigues	
	3.1.18		Party of 2 N.C.O.'s & 8 men Parade at 4.6 P.M. for Rum. Remainder Paraded at 10.0 A.M. for Inspection & General Fatigues. 2.0 P.M. Cleaning Lines.	
	4.1.18		Party of 3 N.C.O's and 4 men Paraded at 7.30 A.M. for work on the lines. Thy rest Cleaning Guns & General Fatigues.	
	5.1.18		Paraded at 10.0 A.M. Inspection & Physical Exercises & General Fatigues. Party of 3 men Paraded 2.0 P.M. to take rations up the line.	
	6.1.18		Paraded at 10.0 A.M. Inspection & General Fatigues. 6 men returned from Trench Mortar Course.	
	7.1.18		Party of 8 men Paraded at 5.0 A.M. for the Line. The rest Paraded at 10.0 A.M. Inspection & General Fatigues.	
	8.1.18		Party of 3 men & 1 N.C.O. Paraded at 5.0 P.M. for the line. rest Paraded at 10.0 A.M. for Inspection & General Fatigues.	

WAR DIARY
or
INTELLIGENCE SUMMARY.
(Erase heading not required.)

Army Form C. 2118.

Place	Date	Hour	Summary of Events and Information	Remarks and references to Appendices
	19.1.18		Party of 4 men & 1 N.C.O Paraded at 7.15 A.M to assist in entraining at H.Q Div. Arty. also a party of 8 men & 2 N.C.O. Paraded at 8.30 A.M. to assist Engineers at H.Q. Div. Arty.	
	20.1.18		Party of 2 men & 1 N.C.O paraded at 8.10 A.M to clean Dug-out at H.Q. Div. Arty. also a party of 2 men & 1 N.C.O. paraded at 9.30 A.M to attend Funeral Parties. and Paraded at 9.45 A.M for C of E Service.	
	21.1.18		Party of 14 men & 1 N.C.O. paraded at 5.30 for the Baths at 11.0 P.M. H. Batley left H.Q. all Ranks attending at New Area at 1.45 P.M.	
	22.1.18		Party of 6 men & 1 N.C.O Paraded for the Baths at 9.A.M. & Remainder General Fatigues and cleaning up new Bell-tents. Parade at 3 P.M. for "Baths"	
	23.1.18		Parade for Inspection at 10.0 A.M. General Fatigues	
	24.1.18		Party of 11 men & 1 N.C.O Paraded at 10 A.M for the Divn.	

WAR DIARY
or
INTELLIGENCE SUMMARY

Army Form C. 2118.

Place	Date	Hour	Summary of Events and Information	Remarks and references to Appendices
	24.1.18		Remainder General Fatigues returned.	
	25.1.18		Parade at 10.0 A.M. for Inspection & General Fatigues. 11 A.M. Parade for Bath.	
	26.1.18		Party of 2 men & 1 N.C.O Parade at 9.00 A.M. for S.A. Tent. Remainder Parade at 10.0 A.M. for Inspection & General Fatigues.	
	27.1.18		Church Parade at 8.45 P.M.	
	28.1.18		Parade for Party of 10 men & 2 N.C.O's at 9 A.M. to General Room Fontanel Remainder Inspection Fatigues & Cleaning Billet.	
	29.1.18		Parade at 10.0 A.M. for Inspection and General Fatigues.	
	30.1.18		Parade at 10.0 A.M. for Inspection and General Fatigues.	
	31.1.18		Parade at 10.0 A.M. for Inspection and General Fatigues. All men returned from the line.	

To/
Brigade Major RA
8th Div Arty

[stamp: TRENCH MORTAR HEADQUARTERS, 8TH DIVL. ARTILLERY
No.......
Date. 1-3-8]

Herewith War Diary
for the month of
February of the
8th Divisional Trench
Mortar Brigade.

E Wagstaff
Capt RFA
DTMO 8th Div

8 D T M Bty
Vol 21

WAR DIARY
INTELLIGENCE SUMMARY

(Erase heading not required.)

Place	Date	Hour	Summary of Events and Information	Remarks and references to Appendices
In the field	1/2/18		Scheme of extensive training, including physical drill, route marches courses of lectures and fatigue parades.	
	2/2/18		The reorganisation of the new T.M. establishment was carried out and the 6" battery now to X/8 and Y/8.	
	3/2/18		Practice for C.R.A's inspection parade which was subsequently cancelled.	
	4/2/18			
	5/2/18			
	6/2/18		Personnel employed in guarding gun emplacements in ST JEAN area. Nine stores one hundred odd and each guarded by an N.C.O. and 3 O.R's. Each position visited daily by an officer.	
	7/2/18			
	8/2/18			
	9/2/18			
	10/2/18			
	11/2/18			
	12/2/18			
	13/2/18		Personnel were from Poperinghe to our area and took over from 292 Siege at VLAMERTINGHE. Y/8 Battery took over the 3 advanced positions at Goudberg Farm, also the advanced positions at Belle Vue	
	14/2/18		One Officer and 25 men attached to 250 Tunnelling Company	

Army Form C. 2118.

WAR DIARY
or
INTELLIGENCE SUMMARY.
(Erase heading not required.)

Instructions regarding War Diaries and Intelligence Summaries are contained in F. S. Regs., Part II. and the Staff Manual respectively. Title pages will be prepared in manuscript.

Place	Date	Hour	Summary of Events and Information	Remarks and references to Appendices
In the field	15/2/18		General fatigues in group & dugouts on the line	
	16/2/18		Officer and O.R's attached to tunnelling company withdrawn. Men not employed in the line on Salvage work.	
	17/2/18		Wiring 2 Archways (cupolas) 2 guns in gun positions. Lentine. Some of the steam laundry.	
	18/2/18		Many G.S wagons from Journal area sent munitions.	
	19/2/18		4/8 Battery relieved by X/83 in the line. Salvage work resumed	
	20/2/18		General fatigues and support in heels of working battery.	
	21/2/18		Intelligence report. Occasional burst of hostile fire on Belle Vue and Manses Cross road F.A. actively normal. Our aircraft very active, many planes crossing and recrossing our front. T.M activity nil on either side.	
	"			
	"			
	22/2/18		Intelligence report. En: fire normal. Enemy batteries & little attention over and to Goudberg Spurs near Belle Vue during the morning Otherwise the day was generally quiet.	
	23/2/18		X/8 Battery relieved X/3 Battery and Salvage work resumed	
			Situation Normal during the day.	

WAR DIARY
or
INTELLIGENCE SUMMARY.
(Erase heading not required.)

Army Form C. 2118.

Place	Date	Hour	Summary of Events and Information	Remarks and references to Appendices
In the field	24/2/18		Intelligence report. Outside fire. Sharp burst of fire on Belle Vue clearing the sleep. E.A. a little active during the afternoon enemies flying over our lines.	
	25/2/18		General fatigues and inspection of new billets and fatigue on the line	
	26/2/18			1/8
	27/2/18		A highly successful shoot was carried out by afternoon T.M.By on enemy T.M. emplacement at V.23.d.55.75. Fire was opened at 6.9 am under cover of a smoke barrage. 35 rounds were fired. Shot observations except for the last few rounds were impossible through the smoke. The results of the last few rounds were however observed on the target and a column of smoke was seen over it some from this point for some considerable time after fire had ceased.	
	28/2/18		Fatigues in the Lines, consisting of ammunition carrying and improvement of posts. Resting battery on R.E. fatigue at Hop Factory.	

S.W. Humphries
Capt. 178 a.
D.T.M.O. 8th Divn.

6 X 8 TM Bty 8

Army Form C. 2118.

WAR DIARY
or
INTELLIGENCE SUMMARY.
(Erase heading not required.)

Place	Date	Hour	Summary of Events and Information	Remarks and references to Appendices
In the field	17/9/15		Cleaning 2" T.M. Guns & Battery cleaning up Bivouac	
	18/9/15		Battery Inspection of arms also General Fatigues	
	19/9/15		Lt. Col. Gray & B.I.O.R'z returned from II Army School of Mortars	
	20/9/15		6 Men & 2 Officers to found posts, Guns in colours the remainder of the Battery in Bivouac except at St Jean.	
	21/9/15			
	22/9/15			
	23/9/15			
	24/9/15			
	25/9/15		Pack & Pick horse being relieved	
	26/9/15		Battery General Inspection Cleaning 6" T.M. Guns also General Fatigues	
	27/9/15		8 N.C.O.s & 22 O.R. working at 2nd Company R.E., nest of Battery General Fatigues	

C. W. Hawkins 2/Lt
X/8 T. M. B.

Army Form C. 2118.

WAR DIARY
or
INTELLIGENCE SUMMARY.
(Erase heading not required.)

Instructions regarding War Diaries and Intelligence Summaries are contained in F. S. Regs., Part II. and the Staff Manual respectively. Title pages will be prepared in manuscript.

Place	Date	Hour	Summary of Events and Information	Remarks and references to Appendices
In the Field	1/2/16		Continuous training	
	2/2/16		"	
	3/2/16		2nd Lt. Gray + 3 O.Rs proceeded to the Army School of Mortars	
	4/2/16		Intensive training	
	5/2/16		"	
	6/2/16		"	
	7/2/16		Guarding gun emplacements in St Jean area	
	8/2/16		"	
	9/2/16		"	
	10/2/16		"	
	11/2/16		"	
	12/2/16		Move to Ness Area by Motor Lorries arrive Ness Area	
	13/2/16		"	
	4/2/16		1 N.C.O. + 12 O.Rs to Tunnelling Co.	
	5/2/16		"	
	6/2/16		1 N.C.O + 12 O.Rs Rt. from Tunnelling Co.	

2353 Wt. W2514/1454 700,000 5/15 D. D. & L. A.D.S.S./Forms/C. 2118.

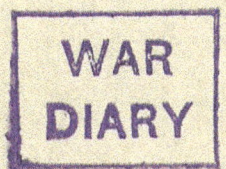

8th DIVISIONAL TRENCH MORTAR BATTERIES, R.A.

M A R C H

1 9 1 8

Army Form C. 2118.

8 D TM Btys
Vol 22

WAR DIARY
or
INTELLIGENCE SUMMARY.
(Erase heading not required.)

Instructions regarding War Diaries and Intelligence Summaries are contained in F. S. Regs., Part II. and the Staff Manual respectively. Title pages will be prepared in manuscript.

Place	Date	Hour	Summary of Events and Information	Remarks and references to Appendices
In the Field	1/3/18		X/8 T.M.Bty in action. 3 offensive patrols at Goudberg Spur and 2 defensive positions at Bette Vae, rest of battery on salvage. X/8 TMBy at VLAMERTINGHE.	
" "	3/3/18		X/8 TMBy relieve Y/8 TMBy in action and remainder of battery relieved at ST JEAN on salvage work. Mortars co-operate in a raid on Tea 12 Coet with Middlesex Regt	
" "	8/3/18		X/8 Bty relieved by 29th Div and Y/8 TMBy took over from 29th Div reserve gun position at ST JEAN.	
" "	10/3/18		General inspection of the 2 gun and ammunition dumps	
" "	14/3/18		Personnel at reserve gun positions relieved by 33rd and 25th Brigades RFA	
" "	15-22/23		Intensive training. Physical training, gun laying, run laying, dipping, musket drill.	
" "	24/3/18		Unofficial visit of C.R.A.	
" "	23/3/18		X/8 TM Bty entrain at Proven our entrain at Marcelcave 24/7/8. Y/8 Bty entrain at Poperinghe enroute for School of Mortars, but owing to the military situation the school was closed down.	
" "	24/3/18		X/8 TMBy proceeds to Gentelucourt. Reported to CRA on arrival of practising Mortars in action	
" "	29/3/18		Left Gentelucourt and proceeded to Inquescourt	

Army Form C. 2118.

WAR DIARY
or
INTELLIGENCE SUMMARY.
(Erase heading not required.)

Place	Date	Hour	Summary of Events and Information	Remarks and references to Appendices
In the Field	27/3/18		Left Inguevrent and proceeded from Aubercourt to Moisel	
"	28/3/18		proceeding to Ailly sur to Noille	
"	30/3/18		from Noille to St Nicholas (Barr)	
"	31/3/18		Summary:—	
			Officers and men of X/5 TM By and Y/5 TM By awaiting	
			R.A.C. Men being attached to OP°1, OP°2, and SAA Sections	
			Also Officers and men assisting in A.R.Ps.	

J.B. Stanplight R.F.C.
L/Com 5th Div

APPENDIX J II

	Officers	OR
Strength on 1st	10	106
Sick	Nil	4
Injured	Nil	1
Re enforcements received	Nil	8
Strength at end of month	10	109

A Steur Capt RTR
for a/OTMO A div

8th Divisional Artillery.

8th DIVISIONAL TRENCH MORTAR OFFICER

APRIL 1918.

To / Staff Capt R.A.
8th Divl Arty

Herewith War Diary
for month of April,
please.

[signature]
Capt R.F.A.
D.T.M.O. 8th Divn

TRENCH MORTAR
HEADQUARTERS,
8TH DIVL. ARTILLERY.
No. T/27
Date 30/4/18

Army Form C. 2118.

WAR DIARY
or
INTELLIGENCE SUMMARY.
(Erase heading not required.)

8DTM 23

Place	Date	Hour	Summary of Events and Information	Remarks and references to Appendices
In the field	1/4/18		Brigade attached to Divisional Ammunition Column from 1/4/18 to 16/4/18	
"	2/4/18		Inspection of arms and general fatigues. 1 officer and 5 other ranks	
"	3/4/18		to A.R.P. — 1 N.C.O. and 3 other ranks to O.R.P. (In bivouac near railway station)	
"	4/4/18		Inspections and general fatigues. 4 ORs to A.R.P. Boxes. Dump shelled and	
"	5/4/18		Brigade moved to Boves. 3 other ranks to A.R.P. men went to haystacks.	
"	6/4/18		General fatigues and cleaning up camp. 3 other ranks to A.R.P.	
"	7/4/18		Inspection of kits, fatigues and 12 other ranks to A.R.P.	
"	8/4/18		Inspection of arms and 13th Respirators. 3/6 TM 13/9 Baths	
"	9/4/18		Fatigues and inspections. 13th Respirators Drill. 3/8 TM 13/9 Baths	
"	10/4/18 11/4/18		18 other ranks sent to A.R.P. or fatigues. Respirators Inspections.	
"	12/4/18		General fatigues. 6 other ranks relieved from A.R.P.	
"	13/14/4/18		Move to Vers staying there one night. All ranks to return from A.R.P.	
"	16/4/18		Move to Cacqueril. Park billets. 3/8 and 3/8 TM 13 Bus grouped separately	
"	17/4/18		Inspection of kits and general cleaning up of new billets. 14	
"	18/4/18		other ranks returned from 29 M.C. Football match with Cycle Corps	
"	19/4/18		Intensive training. Physical Exercises. Marching Drills. Semaphore	

WAR DIARY
or
INTELLIGENCE SUMMARY

Army Form C. 2118.

Place	Date	Hour	Summary of Events and Information	Remarks and references to Appendices
In the Field	19/4/18		Bat Reveilles drill and Rifle drill.	
"	20/4/18		Morning parades and Lecture on Reception and Compensation during the afternoon. Surprise Gas Alert given - good result.	
"	21/4/18		Cleaning up of lines and Church Parade. Half Holiday.	
"	22/4/18		Intensive Evening Visual Signalling. N.C.Os. Mess meeting and lecture on Gas and Esprit de Corps. Supplies of Ammunition	
"	23/4/18		General Inspection Parade by C.R.A. Officers and O.Rs' reconnaissance with view of finding 4 T.M. positions to fire on Tremaires Shet 57E Western half	
"	24/4/18		Intensive Training Kit and Arms inspection. Lecture on the enemy.	
"	25/4/18		Cleaning and inspection of lines. Church Parade. Half Holiday.	
"	26/4/18		V/5 TM 134 medal parade X/5 TM 134 - Rifle and revolver practice on range.	
"	27/4/18		wander Infantry Sergeant Instructor	
"	28/4/18		X/5 TM 134 casual parade. Y/5 TM 134 Rifle and revolver practice on range.	
"	29/4/18		Lecture on Yellow Cross Gas and explanatory details of how to counteract its effects. Model T.M. range in Officers Mess completed.	

Capt R.F.A.
19TMB 8th Divn.

WAR DIARY or **INTELLIGENCE SUMMARY**

Army Form C. 2118.

8^A D/7 T.M. B^ie
May 1918

Vol 24

Place	Date	Hour	Summary of Events and Information	Remarks and references to Appendices
Bray LES	1st		Intensive training	
MAREUIL	2nd		Guns drawn from Park Bery stores Indress	
	3rd		Training	
	4th		Intensive training. Capt R.H. Rudler joined TMB	
	5th		Moved by lorry to SALEUX for entrainment	
	6th		Entrained II A Brigade & TMB at SALEUX	
	7th		Entrained the II A Brigade at SALEUX Intrained	
			Detrained at FERE-EN-TARDENOIS and moved	
			by lorry to BRANGES	
	8th		Intensive training	
	9th		Gun attached to Gun HQ for days awaiting repair	
	10th		Intensive training	
	11th		Intensive training	
	12th		Intensive training	
	13th		Moved by lorry to POUCY, HQ of A/A Battery with	
			the exception of our N.Co for duty & ammunition	

WAR DIARY
or
INTELLIGENCE SUMMARY.
(Erase heading not required.)

Army Form C. 2118.

Place	Date	Hour	Summary of Events and Information	Remarks and references to Appendices
ROUEZ	13th		dumps to shell	
"	14th		Reconnoitred the right water for position	
"	15th		Reconnoitred the centre water for position	
"	16th		Reconnoitred the left water for position	
"	17th		Reconnoitred position on battle line	
"	18th		moved from Rouy to LA PLATRERIE but dumps derailed.	
LA PLAT RERIE	19th		1 Officer and 12 men started to prepare position in centre water.	
"	20th		2 Officers & 20 men started to prepare position in left water.	
"	21st		Work right progressing favourably men billeted properly and fed	
"	22nd		Work progressing. One foot on right water nearly finished.	
"	23rd		Two foot in centre water nearly completed. Two feet of left water nearly completed.	

WAR DIARY
or
INTELLIGENCE SUMMARY
(Erase heading not required.)

Army Form C. 2118.

Place	Date	Hour	Summary of Events and Information	Remarks and references to Appendices
	24th		Both positions on left sector completed reverements camouflage anything anywhere completed. Positions in center & left sector nearly completed	
	25th		50 rounds of ammunition sent up to center sector. Positions in left sector completed	
	26th		50 rounds of ammunition sent up to left sector and 40 rounds to right sector. 2 Forward officers brought up. 2 trench 7 mo.6 which & fell the 2 french positions in center sector	
	27th		Opening of enemy attack. All ammunition at positions fired out the advancing enemy army. 2 nd Lt Kellogg & 2 nd Lt wounded on my Lt center. 2 nd Lt Hunt wounded & one left until 9/Lt MacGing & 6 men missing from left side. Capt A. J. Marsh & twenty missing at his center. At 7.30 it was attempted to get up 2 mule with ammunition	

WAR DIARY
or
INTELLIGENCE SUMMARY.

Army Form C. 2118.

Place	Date	Hour	Summary of Events and Information	Remarks and references to Appendices
	28th		to cover PONTAVERT bridges, owing to shortage of ammunition, inability to get the few remnants available to the position then had to be abandoned after the bridge had been blown up. 12 men, 1 officer killed, missing and must have been captured or driven away to bring amt up Cpr Burton VCO missing from men at OC. The remainder of batteries were then withdrawn	
	29th		to JAC and remained with JAC	
	30th		Both batteries with JAC	
			Both batteries with JAC	

Army Form C. 2118.

WAR DIARY
or
INTELLIGENCE SUMMARY.
(Erase heading not required.)

8 R T M Bay

Place	Date	Hour	Summary of Events and Information	Remarks and references to Appendices
MARNE DISTRICT	1/6/18		Company paraded at B.Hq sheets & blankets inspected	
Doulens	17/4/16		Parades for P.T & G	
NIEPPE FOREST			Picture parade verified and one section to R.P. Dump. L.G. & R.Hq paras to no 1 wing. Pl. Sgt. Darling no 65 x 85. 1st Pl returns early to 11.35. 2 P.G. Serjeants Peter x 5. 2nd Pl Drivers pots to 4.45. 30 more two driver to 4.5. 3rd P.R's two hour parade not 3 Bqn leaves Dept. en road 4.4. P.R's to 9.85	
	19/4/19		Cleaning up and packing up (A.M 0:0). Brig. Brenig Brest A.A. for transport leaving camp at 4	
	19/4/19		Officers and men ready no road in full marching order to Lys Front area 12-8-Point now reach from river ends Dh H Pickets and T. B. Lens. M.Bq. B.Hq. W.T.P. Div to 6th Div and 9 P Lys en road.	

WAR DIARY
or
INTELLIGENCE SUMMARY.
(Erase heading not required.)

Army Form C. 2118.

Place	Date	Hour	Summary of Events and Information	Remarks and references to Appendices
BOULTER ALTRATIOS	21/6/16		Guns complete (6 Trench Battery) Guns Nos LISHERVEL No 82203 4/187 Shewing T No 72365 Gn Baxter T 73260 etc. Reported Firmament military Landing on Submarine to H.Q.M.G.	
	22/6/16		Carriage Training. Capture of Sentine R Gun.	
	23/6/16		Returned for Guns to SUBMARINE. I knew the work of Line Battery ABN outposts I have been nothing excellent ... kit in a first Eng. DEIP ... serving ... Bde limitier ... position at Em BRAGUES.	
EMBRE VISEE	24/6/16		Advance party 4- Aircraft look to air especially Gun Orb Janing. Machine Guns Mysciael Works had Rising Col 12R0 5 founption Commenced in Moses nicestyline.	
	25/6/16		Intensive Sam ...	
	26/6/16		Battles and other drafts of 3rd army in Brigadeer Sgt Saren of 7 & 5 afforted to act as Sgt Major of the Unit.	

Instructions regarding War Diaries and Intelligence Summaries are contained in F. S. Regs., Part II. and the Staff Manual respectively. Title pages will be prepared in manuscript.

WAR DIARY
or
INTELLIGENCE SUMMARY.
(Erase heading not required.)

Army Form C. 2118.

Place	Date	Hour	Summary of Events and Information	Remarks and references to Appendices
[illegible]	26/8/18		2nd Sgt. Turner [illegible] appointed as acting Quartermaster Sgt.	
	27/8/18		Intensive training. Some equipment and clothing commenced coming in, ~~and~~ enabling BCs to start re-equipping their batteries.	
	28/8/18		Intensive training	
	29/8/18		Intensive training. Sgt. F.W. [illegible] awarded Military Cross and No. [illegible] Sgt. Shufflebotham T. awarded Distinguished Conduct Medal for gallantry in action on the [illegible]	
	30/8/18		Intensive training.	
			[illegible] Lt Col R.A. [illegible] 8th [illegible]	

D. D. & L., London, E.C.
(A10266) Wt W5300/P713 750,000 2/18 Sch. 52 Forms/C2118/16.

TRENCH MORTAR
HEADQUARTERS,
8TH DIVL ARTILLERY.

No. T.M.H.Q. 7

Army Form C. 2118.

8th Divisional Trench Mortar Brook

WAR DIARY
or
INTELLIGENCE SUMMARY.
(Erase heading not required.)

Instructions regarding War Diaries and Intelligence Summaries are contained in F. S. Regs., Part II. and the Staff Manual respectively. Title pages will be prepared in manuscript.

Place	Date	Hour	Summary of Events and Information	Remarks and references to Appendices
Enbval	1st		Infantry training Col Tunney O. 9a Class inspected personnel & clothing	
do	2nd		& go into at the circuit	
do	3rd		Infantry training	
do	4th		C.R.A. inspected billets	
do	5th		General Inspection (Brig-Gen. Fell)	
do	6th		Infantry training	
do	7th		do	
do	8th		do	
do	9th		do	
do	10th		do	
do	11th		do	
do	12th		do	
do	13th		do	
do	14th		do	
do	15th		do	Lieutenant R. Clarke joined
do	16th		do	General Inspection (Major General O.C.) 9. a.c.
do	17th		do	Left Enbval ---- at 6 P.M. (Headqrs. by motor transport)
			Entrained at Epinette 6.30 P.M. arrived Somerfort 1 am & went into	billets for night
			amongst 112 ---- by motor transport	
Cavlus	19th		Infantry training	
"	20th		"	
"	21st		Left ---- for the line	
Vimy	22nd		In actors }	26 officers 20 min
"	23rd			to } 527 m.s.
"	24th			{ Battery occupying well improving positions

Army Form C. 2118.

Army Form C. 2118.

WAR DIARY
or
INTELLIGENCE SUMMARY.
(Erase heading not required.)

Place	Date	Hour	Summary of Events and Information	Remarks and references to Appendices
Chimal	25th		1st At trace X Battery improving positions (Y Battery in taking up positions)	
"	26th		2 officers and 2.5 men sent up as working party	
"	27th		Batteries in same positions	
"	28th		" 4 par from hosp last 24 hours	
"	29th		" three relieved	
"	30th			
"	31st		12 June 29 men Duty up to wheel	

8th Divisional Trench Mortar Brigade 1 C.L.

Army Form C. 2118.

WAR DIARY
or
INTELLIGENCE SUMMARY.
(Erase heading not required.)

Instructions regarding War Diaries and Intelligence Summaries are contained in F.S. Regs., Part II. and the Staff Manual respectively. Title pages will be prepared in manuscript.

Place	Date	Hour	Summary of Events and Information	Remarks and references to Appendices
Ypres	1st		In action working in Poitiers	
	2nd		do	
	3rd		do	
	4th		do Officer 14 men went up to the lines	
	5th		do to take ammunition	
	6th		do	
	7th		do one Officer 3.14 men went up to relieve party	
	8th		do working on new positions	
	9th		do	
	10th		do	
	11th		do 1 Officer relieved	
	12th		do 1 Officer 6 men a relief party	
	13th		do	
	14th		do	
	15th		do 2 Officers working	
	16th		do 14 men as relief party	
	17th		do working on new defence positions	
	18th		do	
	19th		do 16 men as relief	
	20th		do Company ammunition dulled how 3 men wounded	
	21st		do	
	22nd		do	
	23rd		do 1 Officer as relief	
	24th		do	
	25th		do	
	26th		do	
	27th		do	
	28th		do 1 Officer and 21 men as relief	
	29th		do relieved 20th Division	

Army Form C. 2118.

WAR DIARY
or
INTELLIGENCE SUMMARY.

(Erase heading not required.)

Instructions regarding War Diaries and Intelligence Summaries are contained in F. S. Regs., Part II. and the Staff Manual respectively. Title pages will be prepared in manuscript.

Place	Date	Hour	Summary of Events and Information	Remarks and references to Appendices
Arsy	29th		In Action	
	30th		do Left Neuville-St-Vaast H.Q. for New T.M.B. Rebecourt	
	31st		do	

Capt R.F.A.
Divisional Artillery

TRENCH MORTAR
HEADQUARTERS.
8TH DIVL. ARTILLERY
No.
Date 31/5/16

WAR DIARY.
AUGUST 1918.
8th Dn. T.M. Bae.

WAR DIARY
or
INTELLIGENCE SUMMARY.
(Erase heading not required.)

Army Form C. 2118.

27th Divisional Trench Mortar Brigade, R.A.

Place	Date	Hour	Summary of Events and Information	Remarks and references to Appendices
Corfu	1st		In action	
	2nd		do	20 Rounds fired
	3rd		do	2 officers went up to sett of
	4th		do	men from 10 Batt did up howard posters
	5th		do	1 officer on relief party
	6th		do	6 men on relief party
	7th		do	2 officers relieved, 2 went on exploration with escort
	8th		do	11 men on fatigue party
	9th		do	
	10th		do	6 men on relief party
	11th		do	One party of men offroare fatigue, 14 men on fatigue
	12th		do	Working on gun positions, 5 vehs, to work on the
	13th		do	Infantry, carrying bombs
	14th		do	and bally on M.M.B. 10R m and 19/M 017
	15th		do	10R mound ready
	16th		do	
	17th		do	Worked with vehicles, and fatigue off 4 men
	18th		do	
	19th		do	Six posters finished
	20th		do	
	21st		do	

Army Form C. 2118.

WAR DIARY
or
INTELLIGENCE SUMMARY.
(Erase heading not required.)

Instructions regarding War Diaries and Intelligence Summaries are contained in F. S. Regs. Part II. and the Staff Manual respectively. Title pages will be prepared in manuscript.

Place	Date	Hour	Summary of Events and Information	Remarks and references to Appendices
6 July	22nd	In Action		
	23rd	do		
	24th	do		
	25	do		
	26	do		
	27	do	6 men on leave/furlo	
	28	do	360 rounds trench mortar ammunition fired during this week	
	29	do		
	30	do		

TRENCH MORTAR HEADQUARTERS,
8TH DIVL. ARTILLERY.
No. ....
Date 30/6/17

R.H. Bagge
Captain R.F.A.
D.T.M.O.
8th Divisional Arty.

Army Form C. 2118.

8th Div: Trench Mortar Brigade R.A.

WAR DIARY
or
INTELLIGENCE SUMMARY.
(Erase heading not required.)

October 1918.

WO 29

Instructions regarding War Diaries and Intelligence Summaries are contained in F. S. Regs., Part II. and the Staff Manual respectively. Title pages will be prepared in manuscript.

Place	Date	Hour	Summary of Events and Information	Remarks and references to Appendices
OPPY	Oct 6		12 batteries in action in OPPY sector. 3 Officers and Gas personnel.	
~do~	7		Solomons was fired at heavily from an aeroplane in Railway Embankment.	
~do~	11		X106 with 39th Infantry in connection with infantry platoon attack withdrawn from area. One battery detailed to remain in action.	
ROEUX	12		On the 12th 2 new T.M. Sergeants left attached to D.A. O.P. became full time action.	
ROEUX			Inst. two strafes and experimental attack. Left FAMPOUX	
			Hqrs. move into FAMPOUX & FRESNES.	
FAMPOUX	13			
FRESNES	15		Two detachments under 2/Lieutenant Gala & Rose Linewetzer & Lieut. Jones have been captured in action.	
	15/16		Special strafe inflicted. Very Boche transverse at 2am.	
	17		On 17 October troops fired all rounds in reserve as OREHEM to up to the west bank of the Canal. Hun by enemy by enemy. Major Stephens - 1/2 Cyr. Burn himself a withdrawn	
	18		Brigade withdrew from OREHEM - 1/2 Cyr. Burn himself a withdrawn on action attachments become as reserve.	
	19		Left FRESNES for PLANQUE.	
PLANQUE	20		Left PLANQUE for CATTELET.	
CATTELET	22		Moved from CATTELET & RONCHELET.	
RONCHELET	26		Two Lieuts & 6 Meters hyres is received, the 3 S.B. Guns with teams of from D.A.C.	

WAR DIARY
or
INTELLIGENCE SUMMARY.
(Erase heading not required.)

Army Form C. 2118.

Place	Date	Hour	Summary of Events and Information	Remarks and references to Appendices
PONCHELET	Oct 27		Reconnaissance carried out with Capt Hotine Liaison had found very dangerous than our own arch'd available elsewhere. Two field engines, Battn H.Q. were at OTOMEZ.	
"	28			
"	30		Moved to MILLONFOSSE.	
MILLONFOSSE	31		30 Rounds fired from where enemy machine gun post was seen flash.	

www.ingramcontent.com/pod-product-compliance
Lightning Source LLC
Chambersburg PA
CBHW080809010526
44113CB00013B/2353